RUDYARD KIPLING

By the same Author

QUEER STREET, 1932
THE ENCHANTED VILLAGE, 1933
TOM TIDDLER'S GROUND, 1934
OLD KING COLE, 1936

❋

POEMS, 1912–1932, 1933

❋

EDGAR ALLAN POE, 1937
MY ENGLAND, 1938

RUDYARD KIPLING
From an Etching by Francis Dodd

RUDYARD KIPLING

A Study in Literature and Political Ideas

by EDWARD SHANKS

COOPER SQUARE PUBLISHERS, INC.
NEW YORK
1970

Copyright © 1940 by Edward Shanks
Published by Permission of Doubleday and Company
Published 1970 by Cooper Square Publishers, Inc.
59 Fourth Avenue, New York, N. Y. 10003
Standard Book No. 8154-0344-5
Library of Congress Catalog Card No. 71-126931

Printed in the United States of America

TO
HERBERT MORGAN

Preface

This book was begun in 1936, shortly after Kipling's death. The writing of it has been continued over the three troubled years which have followed and it was finished shortly before the outbreak of the present war.

It has seemed to me, reading the proofs after making sure that my curtains have been properly drawn, that there is nothing in it which I should qualify in the light of recent events. Kipling's attitude today would be what it was in 1914, though his heart might be heavier. His hope for the world was not destroyed as he grew older but it became more of a long-term hope, and what has happened since his death would have made him think of a longer term.

But, since he was so much misinterpreted during his lifetime, I cannot avoid making a last effort to

Preface

ensure, so far as is possible, that he is not misinterpreted after his death on account of anything I have said of his political ideas. He was an authoritarian. He believed that the man who knows his job should be in a position to give orders to the man who knows less — in so far as that particular job is concerned.

But, as I have pointed out in my last chapter, his faith did not make him a friend of the modern dictatorship. No one can read his "A.B.C." stories, let alone the full range of the Indian stories, without realising how fierce would have been his comtempt of the doctrine of a race called to supremacy by something inherent in its blood. He did believe in the "strong man ruling alone", but the first thing he required in this ruler was a sense of the sacredness of the laws of civilisation — the sacredness of order, peace, plenty and all that may go towards making the interference, indeed the very existence, of the ruler unnecessary.

Kipling's greatness as an artist gave him a peculiar position among those who have propagated political ideas. He was rather like the child in his very early story, *Tods' Amendment*. He lived close to the ordinary men and women whom legislators are apt to regard from a distance. The wealth of detail with which he presented his observations and deductions is frequently confusing and sometimes misleading.

Preface

But there is a wealth of wisdom in it of which more formal political thinkers should take account as the Legal Member of the Viceroy's Council took account of Tods' report of what Ditta Mull, and Choga Lall, and Amir Nath and the other *lakho* of his friends had told him in the bazars about the Sub-Montane Tracts *Ryotwary* Revised Enactment.

It is especially to be emphasised that Kipling's value for us, as a source of political ideas, and, I will add, of fundamental political *information*, such as only a poet can supply, would not be so great but for the later period of his life in which he taught himself all he could about England and her history.

. . . . . .

I have to express my thanks to Kipling's literary executors and to his publishers for the courtesy with which they have allowed me to quote from his works in the pages which follow.

E. S.

December 1939

Contents

I	INTRODUCTION	1
II	THE PREPARATION	17
III	THE PROPHET OF EMPIRE	69
IV	THE FIRST MATURITY	116
V	THE PROPHET OF EMPIRE IN DEFEAT .	171
VI	THE GOLDEN YEARS	191
VII	SUNSET AND AFTER-GLOW	232

RUDYARD KIPLING

CHAPTER I

Introduction

SOME YEARS AGO, in an exhibition of caricatures by Mr. Max Beerbohm, there was one expressing a rarely displayed side of an amiable nature. It represented Rudyard Kipling in the shape of a small, rather tarnished Oriental brass image, standing, apparently forgotten, in the dust at the back of an old-junk shop. The title of this picture was *On the Shelf*. I recall it, not out of a desire to quarrel with Mr. Beerbohm, but because its implications lead direct to a problem which must be faced by anyone who attempts to estimate Kipling's place in English life and literature.

Mr. Beerbohm is not by temperament an acrimonious man. No one who knows him or his work would say that he is given to hatreds. Nothing could be more unlike his usual good-nature than

Rudyard Kipling

public rejoicing over the fall of a fellow-author from the heights of popularity. (Indeed, if Kipling had so fallen, I doubt whether this caricature would ever have been made.) Yet something very like hatred is expressed in every line of the drawing and not least in the obvious and relishing injustice of the title of it.

Nor does it stand alone in Mr. Beerbohm's work. There is an earlier caricature showing Kipling with "his girl Britannia", on a Bank Holiday on Hampstead Heath, which is full of the same spirit. They have exchanged hats. Kipling has Britannia's helmet and she has his bowler — and the total effect is unmistakeably malevolent.

Again — the double parody, both of prose and of verse, in *A Christmas Garland* is by a long way the most brutal thing in that gentle and friendly book. This is an extract from *Police Station Ditties:*

> Then it's collar 'im tight,
>   In the name of the Lawd!
> 'Ustle 'im, shake 'im till 'e's sick!
>   Wot, 'e *would*, would 'e? Well,
>   Then yer've got ter give 'im 'Ell,
> An' it's trunch, trunch, truncheon does the trick.

What is it that makes this dark passion in a breast normally overflowing with kindness towards

Introduction

friends, courtesy towards strangers and tolerance towards enemies? If we could answer that question fully and fairly we should have gone a long way towards discovering what it is that makes Kipling's career so curious a study in the natural history of reputations.

The first entries in this remarkable history of a case go back very nearly to Kipling's beginnings as an author. It was in the early 'Nineties that Wilde said, "As one turns over the pages of his *Plain Tales from the Hills,* one feels as if one were seated under a palm-tree reading life by superb flashes of vulgarity. From the point of view of literature, Mr. Kipling is a genius who drops his aspirates." From the point of view of literature, one might say that Wilde, as a professed stylist, ought to have seen that the very shape of his sentence, apart from any other consideration, demanded the word "aitches" instead of the word "aspirates".

But this was only one of the things which made dubious the reception given to Kipling by critics who were not prepared to deny his genius. In the last year of the 19th century, Richard le Gallienne paid the young author of thirty-five the compliment of writing a book about him, in which he said that, "For the most part Mr. Kipling's work is an appeal to, and a vindication of, the Englishman as brute". He said also:

Rudyard Kipling

His work nobly enforces those old-fashioned virtues of man which, it is to be hoped, will never go out of fashion — to do one's duty, to live stoically, to live cleanly, to live cheerfully. Such lessons can never be taught too often, and they are of the moral bone and fibre of Mr. Kipling's writing. But with them go all the old-fashioned vices of prejudiced Toryism. For progressive thought there has been no such danger in England for many years. Of all that our best poets, philosophers, and social economists have been working for, he is directly, or indirectly, a powerful enemy.

Let us call one more witness out of, roughly speaking, Kipling's own generation. Thirty-odd years ago, Sir Arthur Quiller-Couch wrote:
The *Recessional* proves that, man of genius that he is, he rises to a conception of Universal Law. But too often he is trying to dodge it with sham-law. . . . He takes a twopenny-halfpenny code as the mood seizes him — be it the code of a barrack or of a Johannesburg Jew — and hymns it lustily against the universal code; and the pity and the sin of it is that now and then by flashes — as in *The Miracle of Purun Bhagat* — he sees the truth.

There was one thing that Wilde, Mr. le Gallienne and Sir Arthur Quiller-Couch had in common. Finding something distasteful either in Kipling's manner or in his political philosophy, they still affirmed (it never occurred to them to try to affirm

Introduction

anything else) that he was an artist of genius, and they recognised his importance and his influence.

But later critics have taken a different view, which is epitomised in Mr. Beerbohm's *On the Shelf*. Mr. le Gallienne and Sir Arthur Quiller-Couch were obviously Liberals when they wrote the words which I have quoted from them. But they wrote before 1906. In that year a great event took place. There was a General Election, a long political age came to an end, and the Liberal Party, which had been out of office, or uncomfortably impotent in office, for twenty years, returned on a flood-tide. Its "powerful enemies", the enemies, according to the prevailing school of thought, "of all that our best poets, philosophers and social economists have been working for", were assumed to have been frustrated for ever.

The opinion grew that Rudyard Kipling was no longer an enemy to be reckoned with and his younger critics, instead of defining his faults, began to deny that he had any merits. Thus, in 1913, a now eminent critic, who was then still a member of the Labour Party, wrote of *Songs from Books:*

> His occasional talent for vigorous rhythms is the only specifically poetical gift he has.... Spiritual inspiration and imaginative vision he lacks completely. ... He is a man who, meant to play the piccolo of the temporal, insists on trying to blow the trumpet of

Rudyard Kipling

the eternal. And every time he blows the trumpet he blows the gaff. The publication of this handsome volume should finish Mr. Kipling's reputation as a poet.

This, of course, is sheer nonsense. The critic who wrote it would (if he could be persuaded to speak about it at all, which is unlikely) admit so much. *Songs from Books* contains, among other pieces which make it nonsense, *The Way Through the Woods*. But this critic was looking though spectacles which if not red were at any rate pink. He was able to avoid seeing in Kipling's poetry what he did not want to see. Kipling had been associated with "prejudiced Toryism". The electors of 1906 had put "prejudiced Toryism" out of business. It was an easy and natural step to the assumption that Kipling's great imposture had been exploded and that his reputation was in fact finished.

With the assumption that he was really "on the shelf" came what might perhaps be called a great outburst of critical silence. It is told by that neglected poetical wit, M. Pierre Lièvre, that a French critic once, when he was asked who was really the greatest poet of France, answered, sighing, "Hélas! C'est Victor Hugo". The English intellectual of the 'Twenties and 'Thirties discussing our greatest living authors, would have mentioned various names but would not have even thought of adding, "And,

Introduction

alas, Rudyard Kipling!" He did not so much as sigh over the author of *The Man Who Would Be King* and *The Way Through the Woods*. He simply, though he might be discussing the art of the short story, talked about something else.

It will be observed that thus early in writing about Kipling I have been obliged to refer to the history of party politics. This is the prelude to a study which I do not wish to write in terms of party politics. The terms themselves are in large measure faded and out of date. Who now remembers, or, remembering, feels, the rancours between Conservatives and Liberals which went back as far as the first Home Rule Bill but which so proliferated and grew in venom between 1906 and 1914?

We have fresher preoccupations and different rancours. But it would be quite impossible not to make politics a great part of any book about Kipling. He himself, no less than his enemies, would have regarded it as a stultification of all he stood for. He was a preacher: of course he was a preacher. He adhered to a political doctrine which was the mainspring of his work.

Like other political thinkers, he did not always succeed in expressing his doctrine in its full purity. He was also, as few other political thinkers have been, a great artist, concerned, with an artist's

Rudyard Kipling

passion, to make a picture of the world as he found it. We must continuously endeavour, though it is not always easy, to distinguish between the things which he records because they happened and the things, ideas, attitudes, to which he gives his deliberate approval. There is a formidable work of disentanglement in front of the critic who attempts to understand Kipling both as an artist and as a factor in the life of his time.

But the first necessity is to make it plain how many critical attacks on, and how much critical neglect of, Kipling the artist have sprung from causes irrelevant to his performances in that capacity. The second is to see what his political ideas really were and to what extent they have been misunderstood.

It is a curious fact that the differences between him and his worst enemies, the Liberals, have seemed at some times and at some points not to be very great. There was, however, an element in him which they hated so much that it blinded them — or almost — to what they might have liked in him. And there was that about them which made it impossible for him to see the points on which they should have been in sympathy. Yet they were, in fact, inevitably and perceptibly, if unwillingly, drawn a little way towards him. Mr.

Introduction

Wells, speaking expressly in the character of a 1906 Liberal, says:

Muddle! I remember myself quoting Kipling:

*All along o' dirtiness, all along o' mess,
All along o' doing things rather-more-or less.*

"We build the state," we said over and over again. "That is what we are for — servants of the new re-organisation."

"Drive the road and bridge the ford" is a good poetical slogan for a Five Year Plan — and up to 1906, and even a little later, it was rather frequently quoted by Liberals of Fabian tendencies who did not see why the Devil should have all the good sayings, even if he had made them himself.

Mr. Wells, in particular, has never been able to get quite away from him. In 1933, in *The Shape of Things to Come,* he took over a hope for the future of the world which Kipling had uttered, in the *Windsor Magazine,* twenty-eight years earlier. This story, *With the Night Mail,* pictures a world which has, with beneficial results, put all its affairs into the hands of the Aerial Board of Control — "Theoretically, we do what we please so long as we do not interfere with the traffic *and all it implies*". This is, in principle, an extremely close anticipation of Mr. Wells's conference of

Rudyard Kipling

scientific and technical workers at Basra in 1965, which was organised by the Transport Union and became the World State. In the same story the alleged imperialist and militarist observes drily that "war, as a paying concern, ceased in 1967". In a sequel of seven years later he says, "One knows vaguely that there is such a thing as a Fleet somewhere on the Planet, and that, theoretically, it exists for the purpose of what used to be known as 'war' ".[1]

In fact, he never belonged to a party. It is surely of high significance that though, on several occasions, he might have had any honour that it was in the power of a Government to bestow, he always refused to accept any honour whatsoever on the ground that he must remain free to criticise any Government. I hope that later I shall be able to explain in detail the grounds on which he would have criticised the Conservative Party, of which he was supposed to be a slavish adherent. Here

---

[1] The influence exercised by Kipling on Mr. Wells, a curious mixture of attraction and repulsion, deserves more space than I can give it here and might well make the subject of a separate study. In *The Sleeper Wakes*, three literary works of our time are mentioned as having survived at the beginning of the twenty-second century. One is Conrad's *Heart of Darkness* and the second Henry James's *The Madonna of the Future*. The third is *The Man Who Would Be King*, which the Sleeper remembers as "one of the best stories in the world". At the same time, Kipling's two stories of the Aerial Board of Control may owe something to Mr. Wells's early scientific romances.

Introduction

a single comprehensive sentence must suffice. He would be moved to oppose any betrayal of the principle of firm and orderly government for the benefit, if not with the consent, of the governed. He thought that such betrayal was much more likely to come from the Liberal side than from the Conservative but he was not certain of it. He was vigilant over both sides. It must be admitted that he was sometimes biassed, that he could not abide the tone of voice in which the Liberals often spoke.

And he was a vigorous, wounding controversialist. What he disliked, that he attacked, with all the power at his command. Beetle as a schoolboy composed a poem which described how Mr. King went to Hell and argued with the Devil on the ground that he was a Balliol man. The mature Kipling, a great writer with a world-wide audience, a deep power of hatred, and a gift of rhetorical invective unmatched in our time, saw the then Sir Rufus Isaacs appointed Lord Chief Justice shortly after the Marconi affair. He wrote *Gehazi:*

> Well done, well done, Gehazi!
>   Stretch forth thy ready hand,
> Thou barely 'scaped from judgement,
>   Take oath to judge the land,
> Unswayed by gift of money
>   Or privy bribe, more base,

Rudyard Kipling

*Of knowledge which is profit
In any market-place.*

He was not less wounding with generalities than with personalities. Side by side with his first story about the Aerial Board of Control, in the same collection, he set *The Mother Hive*, that scalding parable of the wax-moth which gets a footing among the bees and brings them to ruin:

"We must disinfect," said a Voice. "Get me a sulphur-candle, please."

The shell of the Hive was returned to its place, a light was set in its sticky emptiness, tier by tier the figures built it up, closed the entrance, and went away. The swarm watched the light leaking through the cracks all the long night. At dawn one Wax-moth came by, fluttering impudently.

"There has been a miscalculation about the New Day, my dears," she began; "one can't expect people to be perfect all at once. That was our mistake."

"No, the mistake was entirely ours," said the Princess.

"Pardon me," said the Wax-moth. "When you think of the enormous upheaval — call it good or bad — which our influence brought about, you will admit that we, and we alone —"

"You?" said the Princess. "Our stock was not strong. So *you* came — as any other disease might have come. Hang close, all my people."

Introduction

When the sun rose, Veiled Figures came down, and saw their swarm at the bough's end waiting patiently within sight of the old Hive — a handful, but prepared to go on.

In the same spirit he conceived the Bandar-Log of *The Jungle Book* and the horse which came as a "walking delegate" to other horses in a Vermont pasture and strove to wake them "to an abidin' sense o' their wrongs an' their injuries an' their outrages". There were certain people, types and individuals, who regarded themselves as architects of progress and whom he regarded as Bandar-Log. He did not hesitate to express his opinion of them and he made it no more acceptable to them by expressing it in an incomparable attacking style.

Let us frankly admit that his hostilities were sometimes waged without discrimination. But those who suffered from them were, however forgivably, unable to discriminate in his work between the controversialist and the artist. And this led to three errors. It led to an all-round condemnation of him in which all sense of values was lost. It led further, naturally perhaps, to two assertions of fact, both of which, I think, are demonstrably quite false. The first was that, since the early years in which his genius had manifested itself to a surprised world, his powers had declined and that the performance of his maturity was unworthy of the promise of

Rudyard Kipling

his youth. Even so acute an observer as the late E. T. Raymond (who had, in fact, very little political prejudice against Kipling) could write in 1919:

> Mr. Kipling came to England about the time of the first great influenza epidemic, and his popularity for long follbwed much the same course as the disease. At first it swept all before it; this devastation was followed by a period of comparative immunity; then the plague returned in somewhat diminished virulence; and since then there have been alternations of ebb and flow, each attack being feebler than the last. The cleanest bill of health, so far as Kiplingism was concerned, synchronised with the Great War. Mr. Kipling is not, perhaps, altogether a spent force. But it seems safe to say that he will never again be more than a minor one.

Now there would have been no matter for astonishment if either or both of these assertions had been true. The precocity of Kipling's genius has been paralleled only three or four times in all the history of literature, and he might well have gone the way of, say, the even more precocious Jean-Arthur Rimbaud. His reputation and his influence, too, sprang up in a moment like the plant from the enchanter's beam. Who could have wondered if so sudden a growth had withered as suddenly?

But it so happened that the young author of *Plain Tales from the Hills* and *Departmental Ditties*

Introduction

had a great deal more than these two books in him. His career is a story of continuous development, amplification and diversification. It could perhaps be argued that there are signs of fatigue in his last collection of stories: that is a question which I shall have to discuss on a later page. It certainly can be argued that the very crown of his work is to be found in *A Diversity of Creatures* and *Debits and Credits*, the two collections which preceded the last. There are some writers who, though they may do other good work, are remembered by common consent especially as men of one (and usually an early) book. It is not so with Kipling. His admirers are easily set off on an argument about the relative merits of *The Jungle Book*, *Kim* and *Puck of Pook's Hill*. If it is a question of his best single story (and, among enthusiasts, discussions on this point may last for several hours), the choices put forward will range over as long a period of time as that which separates *The Man Who Would Be King* and, say, *Friendly Brook* or *The Wish House*.

If his genius did not fail, neither did his influence decrease. The English-speaking peoples continued to read him and there is no present indication of their ceasing to do so. This is a fact, however much anyone may like or dislike it. It is true that his last collection of stories met with a marked falling off in response. But, in my judge-

Rudyard Kipling

ment, that is due to the fact that he was attempting something too difficult for many of his readers and almost, perhaps, for himself. Here again I must refer the reader to a later page. But the popularity of his other work has not been in the least affected. Kipling is still read, and read widely and with pleasure, and therefore, since he is essentially a man with a doctrine to preach, has a formative effect on innumerable minds. He is a great artist. He is a political philosopher with a passionate belief in his own conclusions and an unsurpassed power in recommending them to the minds of others. Because he is both these things he is an historical force which we ought to endeavour to evaluate in all its aspects.

CHAPTER II

The Preparation

JOSEPH RUDYARD KIPLING (his schoolfellow, Beresford, vouches for the first name) was an example of a phenomenon not unknown in the history of genius — a peak rising from a plateau of respectable altitude. His father, John Lockwood Kipling, was a man of at least very great talent. It may be that his one book, *Man and Beast in India*, would not now be remembered if it were not for the fame of his son. But if that were so, it would make only one more addition to the melancholy list of proofs that good books are at the mercy of chance. It is a very good book indeed, as much alive today as when it was written, full of wisdom and humour and vivid description.

Lockwood Kipling was appointed Professor of Architectural Sculpture in the University of Bom-

Rudyard Kipling

bay just in time for his son to be born in that city on December 30th, 1865. His wife, Alice Macdonald, was one of five sisters, the daughters, as her husband was the son, of a Wesleyan minister. Of the other sisters, one married Sir Edward Burne-Jones, a second Sir Edward Poynter, and a third Alfred Baldwin, the father of Lord Baldwin of Bewdley. The young Rudyard (thus named after the place where his parents spent their honeymoon) was born into a family circle no less remarkable than that, say, of the Huxleys and the Arnolds. It is obvious to what influences he was exposed in early days. One of the friends of the circle was William Morris. Kipling remembered how once, when he was staying in the holidays with the Burne-Joneses, Morris appeared in the nursery and, sitting astride a rocking-horse, tested the Saga of Burnt Njal by telling it in his own way to an audience of children.

One of Kipling's biographers has wondered whether, if he had never revisited the country which he left for the first time before he was six, India would have played as important a part in his work as it did. The answer seems to be that it would probably have been very important. Impressions made at that age often seem for a time to have been lost but revive themselves later with great force. Apart from that, the influence of his

The Preparation

parents would have told. This is a point to which we shall have to return. But for a child with a memory so retentive of impressions there was material everywhere. It is certain that from 1871 onwards future stories were beginning to form themselves in his mind. Lockwood Kipling proceeded from his professorship at Bombay to the Curatorship of the Lahore Museum. It was a congenial post, but it meant that the young Rudyard's parents would be staying in India for a long time and that he must be brought up in England apart from them.

At first he was placed with relatives at Southsea. It is a conclusion which many readers must have formed, and which is now not open to guessing that this experience was responsible for *Baa-baa, Black Sheep* and the early chapters of *The Light That Failed*. In both we have a picture of a lonely, difficult but well-natured child, and, in the first, of a child with abnormally bad eyesight.

In his posthumous memoirs Kipling has told us that this fairly obvious guess is even closer to the truth than one might have supposed. But there is no doubt that his story-teller's mind always played with the facts as it pleased. So far as I am aware there is no other account now available of the childhood years. But when we come to boyhood experiences there is a bewildering, four-

Rudyard Kipling

handed conflict of evidence. At the United Services College, at Westward Ho! in Devonshire, Kipling had two close friends whom, in *Stalky & Co.*, he described as M'Turk and Stalky. The first of these, who died not long after Kipling, was G. C. Beresford. The second is Major-General Dunsterville, famous for a great adventure in Central Asia at the end of the War. Each of them holds one of the hands in this peculiar game. The others are held respectively by the Kipling who wrote *Stalky & Co.* and the Kipling who wrote *Something of Myself*. Only one thing emerges as certain and that is that not all four of them can be giving a strictly accurate picture of life at the United Services College. It seems little less certain that no one of them is.

Both Beresford and General Dunsterville have made public their recollections of their old schoolfellow. General Dunsterville takes the line that the memories of old men are unreliable and, as a second and stronger line of defence, — what can it matter now? He is quite clear that he and the other two occupants of Study Five were never the triumphant buccaneers of *Stalky & Co.* He confesses:

Where I am mentioned, faint echoes stir the recording apparatus in my brain, and I have a feeling that even I may have been something like one of the char-

The Preparation

acters depicted, but not on quite so grand a scale. After all, we were only just a lot of potty little schoolboys with playful ingenuity perhaps rather unusually highly developed.

Beresford, confirming this view, emphasises it rather more and adds to it. He is not only anxious to show that he and his study-mates were very commonplace little boys as regards their importance among their fellows. He is anxious also to show that the United Services College was a very "potty" school, that it was, on balance, a rather mean and sordid educational establishment. "It was started", he says, "by some Army and Navy Service people, who, through the niggardliness of fortune, had to look on both sides of a shilling." There is an echo of this fact in the remark, made in *Stalky & Co.* by one of the prefects, that "we aren't a public school. We're a limited liability company paying 4 per cent." (Did they pay that, by the way? If so, it must have been an excellent investment in those days, especially if the shareholders could always depend on prefects so anxious to protect their interests.)

The question is complicated by rather absurd disputes on points of detail. There is some obscure trouble about the use of the Greek Testament as an instrument of instruction at Westward Ho! Could Beetle have dropped a solitaire marble out

Rudyard Kipling

of his choir-boy's robe on the tiles of the chapel-aisle? These problems may be capable of solution, but the evidence is at present inextricably confused. Kipling, in *Stalky & Co.*, writes about fags, and Beresford objects that the institution of fagging did not exist at the United Services College. From this I deduce only that "fag" may have been the term of address used there by an older to a younger boy. (At my own school, where also there was no fagging, a lordly "Here, boy!" was the apostrophe conventionally used by senior to junior.) One thing is easily established and that is that, neither in *Stalky & Co.* nor in his memoirs, does Kipling show any traces of fagging as an organised system of compulsory service rendered by juniors to seniors.

These points may be considered as trivial. There is a good deal more of importance in Beresford's rather sour desire to represent the school as mean and sordid. He conveys the suggestion that it had to obtain its masters as cheaply as possible, and therefore employed some at least who would not have been employed anywhere else. Beetle, of course, made Prout his butt: Beresford makes of him an uncouth lout, almost a half-wit. He holds a low opinion even of the headmaster, Cormell Price, of whom he says that he "took no honours at Oxford, either with his head, or his arms, or

The Preparation

his legs", and that "he was not a strong, masterful man, and had to put up an appearance of strength and determination, a parade of bluff, that one could see was rather a strain on his nerves". He adds the suggestion (which is never made without offensive intention) that "the Prooshian Bates" wore a beard to conceal an unimpressive chin.

Here the Kipling of the autobiography may be cited for a comment which is probably not irrelevant:

Turkey possessed an invincible detachment — far beyond mere insolence — towards all the world: and a tongue, when he used it, dipped in some Irish-blue acid. Moreover, he spoke, sincerely, of the masters as "ushers", which was not without charm.

I have no information regarding Beresford's antecedents or subsequent career which throws any light on the unexplained fact of his having been at the United Services College at all. It does not appear that he had any Service connections or ambitions. As a character of fiction he is described as "viceroy of four thousand naked acres, only son of a three-hundred-year-old house, lord of a crazy fishing-boat, and the idol of his father's shiftless tenantry". It may well be that his grievance against the school springs from some sense of misplacement.

Rudyard Kipling

Against his judgement of the masters, we may quote again from *Something of Myself:*

My main interest as I grew older was C——, my English and Classics master, a rowing-man of splendid physique and a scholar who lived in secret hope of translating Theocritus worthily. He had a violent temper, no disadvantage in handling boys used to direct speech, and a gift of schoolmaster's "sarcasm", which must have been a relief to him and was certainly a treasure-trove to me.... I wish I could have presented him as he blazed forth once on the great Cleopatra Ode – the 27th of the Third Book. I had detonated him by a very vile construe of the first few lines. Having slain me, he charged over my corpse and delivered an interpretation of the rest of the Ode unequalled for power and insight.

The man whose interpretation of an Ode of Horace was remembered by Kipling, after fifty-odd years, as "unequalled for power and insight" was clearly no ordinary man. But here at once we encounter another tangle in the evidence. This C—— is, beyond doubt, the King of *Stalky & Co.*, and no such praise is apportioned to him in that book. The tangle is still further twisted by a story, *Regulus*, which Kipling wrote in his later years as an appendix to the earlier series but which takes a very much more favourable view of King. And yet again there is another late ad-

The Preparation

dition, *The Propagation of Knowledge*, containing the decidedly unfriendly phrase, "a happy and therefore not too likeable King".

Of course Kipling is not to be held too strictly to account in a series of short stories about school-life, even though he took no pains to prevent identification of the school itself and of the chief characters in the stories. He was writing fiction and, as we shall have more than one occasion to see later, he was able to make a little fact go a long way in fiction. But, since we are discussing the influences which made him, we want to get at as much fact as we can.

But there are more contradictions than these. Beresford records this as his first impression of the twelve-year-old Kipling:

When you looked more closely at this new boy, you were astonished to see what seemed to be a moustache right across the smile; and so it was — an early spring moustache just out of the ground of his upper lip. Kipling's hair being dark, the moustache was visible, when you had twigged that it really was a moustache, from quite a number of feet off. It was not actually against regulations for lower-school boys to wear moustaches, but it looked like trespassing on the privileges of the prefects and the upper sixth, who could — if able and so disposed — display some faint pencilling on the upper lip. However it was not advisable to order the new arrival to shave, so the matter was passed over.

What Kipling says does not precisely contradict this but is certainly not congruent with it. He says that in his last term his chin became so offensively hairy that C——(that is to say, King) could bear it no longer and took steps which led to the young Kipling's house-master giving him "a written order on a Bideford barber for a razor, etc." This is a not uncommon experience for schoolboys in the last term or earlier, and does not bear out the suggestion of extraordinary physical precocity which Beresford suggests. He, by the way, prints a sketch of the moustached schoolboy, made, he says, at the time. It represents the moustache as being almost as heavy as that which Kipling used to wear in mature years and might be used in support of the often repeated legend that he had "country-blood" in him. Of the truth of this legend I have never been able to find any evidence whatsoever. And, let me add, I should like some further assurance that this and some other drawings in Beresford's book were really made at the time.

There is yet one more important point in which Beresford's picture differs from Kipling's own. Beetle assigned to himself a relatively humble

The Preparation

place in the exploits of the three and in public esteem generally. Beresford makes him a leader and a power in the school in virtue of his wide knowledge and natural wisdom. There is a reason which could be suggested for this — but perhaps I have said enough about Beresford's narrative already.

These investigations throw a somewhat chilling light on the conclusions of history. Here we have a wealth of evidence for the boyhood of a great man. We have two accounts from his own hand, one written while he was in his thirties, the other when he was approaching seventy. They differ palpably, and the testimonies of his closest friends at that time, while they do not agree at all points, do agree in emphasising the difference.

Such matters are not unimportant. Sometimes we are left in doubt concerning the early years of great men for sheer absence of evidence. We do not know, and probably never shall, what was the illness which was nearly the end of Goethe when he was at Leipzig. Mr. B. W. Matz pauses in the midst of his copious annotations on Forster's Life of Dickens to lament that we cannot tell when, where or how Dickens learnt to ride — and if to Mr. Matz this is an unanswerable question, then it is likely to remain unanswered for ever. We ought not to have these gaps in our knowledge of Kipling.

Rudyard Kipling

But it would seem that already his schooldays, less than sixty years ago, are obscured by trailing clouds of uncertainty.

There are, however, certain conclusions which we can accept with confidence. One is that there never were any such schoolboys as Stalky, Turkey and Beetle. Kipling establishes that fact in *Something of Myself*, in the one story he tells of the joint action of the three:

> We had been oppressed by a large toughish boy who raided our poor little lockers. We took him on in a long, mixed rough-and-tumble, just this side of the real thing. At the end we were all-out (we worked by pressure and clinging, much as bees "ball" a Queen) and he never troubled us again.

This is a long way from the grand strategic combinations of *Stalky & Co.* (But there never was, for that matter, such a wolf-boy as Mowgli.)

The second is one which we can accept without hesitation as we find it in *Stalky & Co.* It is that Cormell Price, to whom the book was dedicated, must have been the ideal headmaster for the young Kipling. He was a minor member of the Pre-Raphaelite group by virtue of his early friendship with Burne-Jones, Kipling's uncle by marriage. Even Beresford, while sneering at him, throws in some expressions of admiration. Assuredly we

The Preparation

need not question what Kipling says of Price's hand in his training. He is writing of the time when the editorship of the College paper was placed in his hands and "the Prooshian Bates":

Gave Beetle the run of his brown-bound, tobacco-scented library; prohibiting nothing, recommending nothing. There Beetle found a fat armchair, a silver inkstand, and unlimited pens and paper. There were scores and scores of ancient dramatists; there were Hakluyt, his voyages; French translations of Muscovite authors called Pushkin and Lermontoff; little tales of a heady and bewildering nature, interspersed with unusual songs — Peacock was that writer's name; there was Borrow's *Lavengro;* an odd theme, purporting to be a translation of something called a "Rubáiyát", which the Head said was a poem not yet come to its own; there were hundreds of volumes of verse. . . . Then the Head, drifting in under pretence of playing censor to the paper, would read here a verse and here another of these poets; opening up avenues. And, slow breathing, with half-shut eyes above his cigar, would he speak of great men living, and journals, long dead, founded in their riotous youth; of years when all the planets were little new-lit stars trying to find their places in the uncaring void, and he, the Head, knew them as young men know one another.

Cormell Price must have thought himself exceptionally lucky in one characteristic of this exceptional case. Kipling, from a very early age, suffered from extremely short sight. "Suffered" is perhaps not the word. It might be better to say that he rejoiced in it. It released him from compulsory games which would have bored him and wasted his valuable time. It did not prevent him from reading or wandering about the countryside or observing the actions of other people, which were the things he most delighted in doing. It did give his headmaster full liberty to treat him as a case out of the ordinary. At the end of his life he wrote: "Looking back from this my seventieth year, it seems to me that every card in my working life has been dealt me in such a manner that I had but to play it as it came". Even when he was still a child he had the luck of the deal in the matter of his eyes and the additional luck of a wise man looking over his shoulder and showing him how to play the first cards.

Not every boy of promise is fortunate enough to have a helpful schoolmaster. Very few have that and a wise father as well. Lockwood Kipling exercised the only influence on his son's early years which was comparable to that of Cormell Price. This influence was necessarily intermittent. But it came into play on one notable occasion, and with powerful effect, before the boy had had time to settle down at the United Services College. In 1878 the father came to Europe in charge of

The Preparation

the Indian Section of the Paris Exhibition and took his son with him to Paris. Long afterwards, in one of the last works published during his lifetime, the son told the story with delightful freshness:

Our happy expedition crossed the Channel in a steamer, I think, made of two steamers attached to each other side by side. (Was it the old *Calais-Douvres* designed to prevent sea-sickness, which even the gods themselves cannot do?) And, late at night, we came to a boarding-house full of English people at the back of the Parc Monceau. In the morning, when I had waked to the divine smell of roasting coffee and the bell-like call of the *marchand-d'habits*, my father said in effect, "I shall be busy every day for some time. Here is——" I think it was two francs. "There are lots of restaurants, all called Duval, where you can eat. I will get you a free pass for the Exhibition and you can go where you please." Then he was swallowed by black-coated officials and workmen in blouses.

Later than this, Lockwood Kipling did his son an even more remarkable service. It was one which, in most cases, most observers would call, and with reason, a foolish paternal indulgence. While the young Rudyard was still at school his father collected the poems which he had enclosed in his "letters home", and had them printed in India in a volume called *Schoolboy Lyrics*. I have

Rudyard Kipling

known something like this to happen two or three times and, in my experience, it has always been ill-advised. Here it was not. The young author was of a temper to appreciate the lesson which is taught to every author, even to the end of his life, when he sees in print what he has written.

It is a remarkable fact that nowhere, so far as I have been able to discover, does Kipling mention the volume at all. Beresford implies that he kept all knowledge of its existence from his schoolfellows, even from the other two occupants of Study Five — which is evidence of extraordinary discretion and restraint in a juvenile poet. To me it seems that Lockwood Kipling chose, with astonishing tact, just the right time and the right way to confirm his son in the path which the stars had marked out for him.

Kipling himself, we may suppose, knew exactly the effect and the purpose of his father's action. In later years he did allow it to be reprinted, though never for general circulation. His failure to say anything about it was not, assuredly, due to any lack of gratitude. He was one of the most naturally grateful men who ever lived. No one who had done him a service, living or dead, did he ever forget. His father, his mother, his sister, Cormell Price and a score more of persons whom he had known alive, with a score of dead authors whom

The Preparation

he had loved and in whose footsteps he had followed, all received the generous acknowledgement of his indebtedness.

The volume which his father had printed makes a fitting close to the unusual story of his childhood and boyhood. It did justify the hopes for his future which were entertained by those who were watching him. Some of the pieces are "schoolboy lyrics" in the strictest sense — for example, a description of his sufferings with tonsillitis. A number are highly derivative, with Browning the main source of inspiration, as in *An Echo*.

> Let the fruit ripen one by one
>   On the sunny wall;
>   If it fall
> Who is it suffers? What harm is done?
>   None at all.
>
> An Eve in the garden am I;
>   Behold this one
>   In the sun
> Falls with a touch, and I let it be,
>   My first one.
>
> One fresh from the bough; I break it,
>   The red juice flies
>   Into my eyes.
> Shall I swallow, leave, or take it,
>   Or despise?

Rudyard Kipling

> Sweet to my taste was that second
>   And I hold it meet
>   That I eat;
>   But ah me! Are the bruised ones reckoned
>   At my feet?

But there is an unmistakable anticipation, of some notes to be sounded by the later Kipling himself, in a genuine "schoolboy lyric":

> Our heads were rough and our hands were black
>   With the ink-stain's midnight hue,
> We scouted all, both great and small —
>   We were a dusky crew;
> And each boy's hand was against us raised,
>   'Gainst me and the Other Two.
> We chased the hare from her secret lair,
>   We roamed the woodlands through;
> In parks and grounds far out of bounds
>   Wandered our dusky crew;
> And the keepers swore to see us pass —
>   Me and the Other Two.

(Here, by the way, is contemporary evidence that Kipling did, during his schooldays, think of himself and his friends as the adventurous outlaws whom he afterwards depicted in *Stalky & Co.*)

At the end of his schooldays there was another and a most significant anticipation. The maturest piece, from a technical point of view, in *Schoolboy Lyrics* is *Ave Imperatrix*, which was called forth

The Preparation

by a madman's attempt on the life of Queen Victoria. In it Kipling sends a message from the United Services College:

> Such greeting as should come from those
>   Whose fathers faced the Sepoy hordes,
> Or served You in the Russian snows,
>   And, dying, left their sons their swords.
>
> And some of us have fought for You
>   Already in the Afghan pass —
> Or where the scarce-seen smoke-puffs flew
>   From Boer marksmen in the grass.
>
> . . . . .
>
> Once more we greet You, though unseen
>   Our greeting be, and coming slow,
> Trust us if need arise, O Queen,
>   We shall not tarry with the blow.

Beresford declares that Kipling wrote this not quite seriously. To my mind, the qualification destroys the force of the judgement. Such things are written either quite seriously or with the whole of the tongue in the cheek. According to Beresford, who tells us also that Cormell Price was a Gladstonian Liberal, Kipling at school was something of an anti-militarist, who once said magisterially that war was not a subject for the poet at all. This may have been due to the influences of his holidays with the Burne-Joneses. However

Rudyard Kipling

that may be, it is conceivable that he converted himself in writing *Ave Imperatrix* or, which is more likely, thus brought to a decisive point a process of conversion which had been going on within him for some time without his being aware of it. For my part, I find the lines too good to be able to believe that they are fundamentally insincere. They can hardly be called original in style — but then Kipling, when he was at his best in verse, was never entirely original, which is not a derogatory judgement. They are in a tone which he was to use again and again in after years, and they are not unworthy of his later use of it. The seventh and eighth of the lines here quoted illustrate very notably his power of sharp visual appreciation of something which in fact he himself had not seen.

This was the schoolboy's climax. It seems to indicate that he had taken the sudden leap forward which boys approaching seventeen often do take. Nothing could have been more fortunate than that now the processes of life should have been fully ready to carry him on into a new stage. He had had for the new stage as good a preparation as human conditions are likely to offer to any young man of genius. Can it be supposed that a better (or more expensive) school, with stricter discipline and possibly more efficient teaching, followed by three or four years at one of the Universities, would

The Preparation

have been of any greater service to him? A discerning and sympathetic schoolmaster close at hand and a discerning and sympathetic family at a distance had, to a very large extent by letting him alone, prepared him to take the opportunity which was bound to come. The talent shown in *Ave Imperatrix* suggests that it would have been futile, and perhaps harmful, to have delayed any longer the entrance into real life. With however much reserve we feel obliged to take some of the details in *Stalky & Co.*, we can believe that Kipling correctly describes the feelings of Beetle after he had been told what his future was to be:

> He was on a steamer, his passage paid into the wide and wonderful world — a thousand leagues beyond Lundy Island.

II

Luck still favoured him and he found it a wonderful world indeed. He was the owner already of an almost formed literary talent, and he was placed in surroundings which gave him the widest possible opportunities for its use. He would not need here to confine himself to lampoons on schoolmasters, to pictures of Mr. King in Hell explaining to the Devil that he was a Balliol man. There were Governors, and Lieutenant-Governors, and even a Viceroy and his

Rudyard Kipling

Council, to be shot at. Nor was it merely such an opportunity as might have been offered to any young man with equivalent gifts who should have taken up a post on an Indian newspaper at that time. Kipling had the memories of his childhood for a background. He had also a devoted family already settled in India and learned in its ways and peculiarities. He was saved a great deal of time during which he might have been making mistakes which would have taken him as long to clear up afterwards. We may express it by saying that he landed on his feet.

We know now that he did not like life in India very much, that quite soon he began to think of ways of escaping from it. But he did like the life of a journalist. All his life he was the good reporter who had, as a moral obligation, to bring in a good story from every experience. One of his editors in India reflected later on the advantages of employing a man who, because he is a genius, is ready to do the work of three men. Kipling probably tried to do the work of four or five or six. There were so many stories in India lying about waiting to be brought in. If he brought in only three out of the possible six it was only because he could not be, even in imagination, in more than three places at once.

This is perhaps the place to speak of the

The Preparation

enormous influence which he has exercised on the practice of journalism in all the English-speaking countries. He had a distinguished disciple, in G. W. Steevens, who did more than anyone else, besides the master, to perpetuate the tradition. But his influence is widely spread. We may fairly say that there is not a famous special correspondent of our times, either English or American, who would give us his impressions just as he does if Kipling, instead of serving that apprenticeship in India, had died on the voyage out.

He never escaped, or sought to escape, from the machine to which he had at the beginning given his energies. He wrote in later years:

> Who once hath stood through the loaded hour
>   Ere, roaring like the gale,
> The Harrild and the Hoe devour
>   Their league-long paper bale,
> And has lit his pipe in the morning calm
>   That follows the midnight stress —
> He hath sold his heart to the old Black Art
>   We call the Daily Press.

As Le Gallienne remarked, the precepts which all reporters are bound to obey are such as all authors may profitably study. They must stick to the point, they must see what is there, and they must make the reader see it too. In journalism, success

Rudyard Kipling

or failure, according to the observance of these rules, follows so hot upon performance that the reporter soon learns a strict discipline which the mere author must laboriously teach himself. The practice of journalism, with its incessant demand for indeliberate haste, may sometimes do harm to the style of a young writer — in the minuter sense of the word "style". A hard grindstone will wear badly tempered steel into rags, but to good steel it will impart a cutting edge.

I have wandered rather deeply into general principles from Kipling, the seventeen-year-old journalist on an English newspaper in India. But the fact remains that the chronological sequence has the heart of the matter in it, and that if we do not consider Kipling first as a journalist we shall understand neither his career nor his genius. And it may be remarked here that what he owed to his profession he generously repaid. Two great English writers of imaginative literature began in the routine practice of journalism. The first was Dickens, the second was Kipling. Both infected their own generations like a fever, both have left their marks behind them even to this day.

In one sense the basis of all Kipling's work was reporting on a gigantic and lavish scale. The world enchanted him, as it should enchant a young

The Preparation

reporter. He wanted to see it all and to make a picture of it. What he could not see for himself, he would see through the eyes of others. He had by nature the reporter's faculty of picking up the significant facts easily and making the most of them. This was one of his primary abilities and he never sought to disguise it. There is something like a proud confession in *The Finest Story in the World*:

"One minute, Charlie. When the sea topped the bulwarks what did it look like?" I had my reasons for asking. A man of my acquaintance had once gone down with a leaking ship in a still sea, and had seen the waterlevel pause for an instant ere it fell on the deck.

"It looked just like a banjo-string drawn tight, and it seemed to stay there for years," said Charlie.

Exactly! The other man had said: "It looked like a silver wire laid down along the bulwarks, and I thought it was never going to break." He had paid everything except the bare life for this little valueless piece of knowledge, and I had travelled ten thousand weary miles to meet him and take his knowledge at second hand.

I do not know the explanation of the "ten thousand weary miles", which sounds rather extravagant. But obviously Kipling spent most of his time in India, and, for that matter, a good deal of his life, eagerly picking up little pieces of knowl-

Rudyard Kipling

edge which would be not without value when he had decided how they could best be used.

Very soon he began to distinguish himself by more than plain newspaper reporting. To the existence of occasional blank columns in the pages of the *Civil and Military Gazette* we owe *Departmental Ditties* and *Plain Tales from the Hills* — and to this Kipling owed his first ascension into fame. He has himself given us a vivid account of how *Departmental Ditties* came to be written:

Bad as they were, I burned twice as many as were published, and of the survivors at least two-thirds were cut down at the last moment. Nothing can be wholly beautiful that is not useful, and therefore my verses were made to ease off the perpetual strife between the manager extending his advertisements and my chief fighting for his reading-matter. They were born to be sacrificed. Rukti-Din, the foreman of our side, approved of them immensely, for he was a Muslim of culture. He would say: "Your potery very good, sir; just coming proper length today. You giving more soon? One-third column just proper. Always can take on third page. . . ."

He also makes a picture of the fun of writing verse in an Indian paper:

Sometimes a man in Bangalore would be moved to song, and a man on the Bombay side would answer him, and a man in Bengal would echo back, till at last

The Preparation

we would all be crowing together like cocks before daybreak, when it is too dark to see your fellow.[1]

There was an obvious link between these *jeux d'esprit* and the Beetle who had written a poem about King in Hell telling the Devil that he was a Balliol man. The English community in India is far-scattered but it is small, and it is as fond of gossiping as any country parish. Witty and pointed comments on events which had, or might have, happened among its members were sure of a receptive audience.

It would be futile now to enquire which of the scandals, ludicrous or tragic, reported in *Departmental Ditties*, really did occur. There cannot be many survivors of the society of Simla at which Kipling laughed with so little reverence or reserve when he was twenty. It does not matter today whether he had a specific instance in mind when he wrote about Potiphar Gubbins, C.E., or was making a modern version of a story that recurs throughout history. To his contemporary readers also it mattered less than they probably thought. But it pleased them to be able to scent a scandal even when they could not name the parties.

We, today, who care nothing about the parties,

---

[1] These extracts are from an article in *The Idler*, quoted by Le Gallienne.

Rudyard Kipling

read *Departmental Ditties* for their vigour and pungency. For the extraordinary thing is that many of these pieces have worn very well. They are still "schoolboy lyrics", no doubt: the compositions of a preternaturally precocious and gifted schoolboy let loose in a gossiping society in which strange things sometimes happened and very strange things were invariably believed. But they are always witty and well-turned and now and again they have a universal application. It was probably true in the more highly organised states of Mesopotamia that:

By the Laws of the Family Circle 'tis written in letters of brass
That only a Colonel from Chatham can manage the Railways of State,
Because of the gold on his breeks, and the subjects wherein he must pass;
Because in all matters that deal not with Railways his knowledge is great.

Like phenomena can be found today, and not only in the Indian Empire, and humanity must change a good deal before they are so unfamiliar that the reader is driven to wonder what Kipling can have meant.

In the verse which he wrote at this time there were undoubtedly vulgarities of the sort often quoted when his later success raised up critics in

The Preparation

England, such vulgarities as the famous "A woman is only a woman, but a good cigar is a smoke" and:

My Son, if a maiden deny thee and scufflingly bid thee give o'er,
Yet lip meets with lip at the lastward. Get out! She has been there before.
They are pecked on the ear and the chin and the nose who are lacking in lore.

These belong to the Kipling who, a little later, with a skilful admixture of sentiment wrote *The Story of the Gadsbys*. They can be dismissed now as so much adroit versification which pleased the readers for whom it was intended. So too, because they are untransplantably rooted in their occasions, can such pieces as *The Rupaiyat of Omar Kal'vin*. We can also, if we choose, describe as relics of apprenticeship the semi-parodies of Browning, *A Tale of Two Cities* and *One Viceroy Resigns*. In the second of these the outgoing Lord Dufferin speaks to the incoming Lord Lansdowne:

So here's your Empire. No more wine, then? Good.
We'll clear the Aides and *Khitmutgars* away.
(You'll know that fat old fellow with the knife —
He keeps the Name Book, talks in English, too,
And almost thinks himself the Government.)
O Youth, Youth, Youth! Forgive me, you're so young,

Rudyard Kipling

Forty from sixty — twenty years of work
And power to back the working. *Ay de mi!*
You want to know, you want to see, to touch
And, by your lights, to act. It's natural.
I wonder can I help you? Let me try.
You saw — what did you see from Bombay east?
Enough to frighten anyone but me?
Neat that! It frightened me in Eighty-four!

This, however, is a piece of admirable versification and diction and of astounding breadth and ripeness of judgement for so young a man.

But beyond these things, good and bad, written in what, for all their positive brilliance of achievement, I choose to call the years of preparation, there is something else to be added. The young Kipling was, as they said, often vulgar, his colours, however artfully laid on, were often garish and crude, he favoured rhythms which sounded like shouting and, above all, there was a cynical knowingness about him which was impressive but not poetical. Yet for *Departmental Ditties* he wrote an envoi:

> The smoke upon your Altar dies,
>   The flowers decay,
> The Goddess of your sacrifice
>   Has flown away.
> What profit then to sing or slay
> The sacrifice from day to day?

The Preparation

"We know the Shrine is void," they said,
   "The Goddess flown —
"Yet wreaths are on the altar laid —
   "The Altar-Stone
"Is black with fumes of sacrifice,
"Albeit She has fled our eyes.

"For, it may be, if still we sing
   "And tend the Shrine,
"Some Deity on wandering wing
   "May there incline;
"And, finding all in order meet,
"Stay while we worship at Her feet."

These were strangely prophetic words, for Kipling was to find the shrine at which he had worshipped deserted by the Deity whom he had sincerely adored, and was to find also that the empty place was in due time filled by another whom he could worship no less sincerely. But it is impossible to think that any such premonition was in his mind when he wrote these lines.

The greatest interest of them is that we find, just as we found in *Schoolboy Lyrics,* an almost uncanny hint of what his style was later to be. It is perhaps worth noting here that they moved Le Gallienne, writing in 1900, to remark that "Mr. Kipling was already tuning his banjo to such purpose that it might even, on occasion, do duty for a lyre". It would have been better to say that he owned a lyre as well as a banjo and was quite capable of using either, according to the subject and his mood.

But possibly, in writing of Kipling, it is better to avoid using musical instruments as illustrations. We have here a lyre and a banjo, and on an earlier page we have already encountered a trumpet and a piccolo. Mr. Max Beerbohm drew him playing a concertina, and my mind at this point throws up a vague memory of something about both mouth-organs and barrel-organs. Later, if I am not careful, I shall find myself saying something about the shepherd's pastoral flute. And it is also most unlikely that no one has ever associated him with a big drum.

III

The *Plain Tales from the Hills,* which found their first excuse for existence in much the same way as *Departmental Ditties,* were of a nature to arouse the same interest in India and at the same time much more likely to recommend their author to a wider world elsewhere. To the English in India they conveyed just the same suggestion of more or less scandalous revelations about their own small, closely interknit society.

The Preparation

Readers in England needed not to have their appetites titillated by the promise of scandal which would have meant nothing to them in any case. What did interest them was this picture of a wholly unfamiliar sort of life. They thought they knew something about India. There were stories of heroism and disaster and triumph in the wars in the Punjab and Afghanistan. There were stories of heroism and suffering in the Mutiny. The names of Clive, Warren Hastings, Havelock, the Lawrences, the Nicholsons, were more or less familiar. But a new life had arisen in India since the Mutiny and of the actual texture of that life the home-staying public knew next to nothing. If it thought at all about the administrators and defenders of the vast and incredible Indian Empire, it thought about them much in the terms of that curious sonnet in Robert Bridges's *The Growth of Love*, which was published in the year after Kipling went to Westward Ho! Bridges, in Florence, saw what were then still properly called Anglo-Indians on their way home:

> Say who be these light-bearded, sunburnt faces
> In negligent and travel-stain'd array,
> That in the city of Dante come today,
> Haughtily visiting her holy places?
> O these be noble men that hide their graces,
> True England's blood, her ancient glory's stay,

Rudyard Kipling

> By tales of fame diverted on their way
> Home from the rule of oriental races.
> Life-trifling lions these, of gentle eyes
> And motion delicate, but swift to fire
> For honour, passionate where duty lies,
> Most loved and loving, and they quickly tire
> Of Florence, that she one day more denies
> The embrace of wife and son, of sister or sire.

It is a little odd to reflect that the author of this poem and the then schoolboy were in later years to be considered by some to be rivals for the position of Poet Laureate. The contrast between Kipling's picture and that given by Bridges, though it is of course in a sense only superficial, was startling. Bridges saw from a distance. Kipling, observing at close quarters and with a not unmalicious eye, presented the "life-trifling lions" in the persons of the admirers of Mrs. Hauksbee and Mrs. Reiver, in the persons of Otis Yeere and Aurelian McGoggin, of Pluffles and Lieut. Golightly — to say nothing of Jack Barratt and Potiphar Gubbins.

This novelty of view soon caught the taste of the English public. *Plain Tales from the Hills* first appeared in India in 1888, and the Calcutta publishers sent a thousand copies to their London house. The traveller whose fate it was to be

The Preparation

ordered to sell this consignment to the trade has described his discouraging experiences. He contrived to sell sixteen copies before publication and the reviewers were not helpful at first — "the first real recognition came from *The Saturday Review* which devoted nearly a column to it. This created a demand from the libraries and other papers followed suit." There then ensued a misfortune which sometimes falls on young authors whose success surprises their own publishers. The stock ran out and for some time could not be replenished. But this did not result in his being forgotten. He had made on those who had had the opportunity of reading him too deep an impression for that. From the arrival in England of this consignment of a thousand copies his success was assured.

I include this book, along with *Schoolboy Lyrics* and *Departmental Ditties*, among the works produced in "the years of preparation". But that is not to say that it is immature, in the sense that it is now kept alive only by its author's later writings. It is indeed remarkably mature and, of its sort, a little masterpiece. The young man might have been forgiven if, in breaking this vitually virgin field, he had at first fumbled a little and produced uneven results. But the forty stories of *Plain Tales from the Hills* cover a cer-

Rudyard Kipling

tain space of ground with great sureness. Not all of British India was in them, but there was certainly as much as any reader at home could reasonably be expected to take in at one time. By no means all of the future Kipling was evident or even implicit in them, but they did make a real book which was solid and durable in its own right. If its author had died on the day after publication, it would still not have been forgotten.

As one looks back on it now, it is impossible not to be surprised by finding in it so many of the characters of whom one naturally thinks as soon as Kipling's name is mentioned. Thus early he showed his liking for the practice of using the same characters in several separate stories, and he introduced here to the world not only Mrs. Hauksbee and Mrs. Reiver but also Mulvaney, Ortheris and Learoyd, all in the compass of a single volume. Mrs. Hauksbee and private Mulvaney are both important members of the British community in India, but at points rather far apart. Nor did Kipling confine himself to such specimens. Another was a bank-manager, admirably sketched:

There were two Burkes, both very much at your service. "Reggie Burke," between four and ten, ready for anything from a hot-weather gymkhana to a riding-picnic, and, between ten and four, "Mr. Reginald Burke, Manager of the Sind and Sialkote Branch

The Preparation

Bank." You might play polo with him one afternoon and hear him express his opinions when a man crossed; and you might call on him next morning to raise a two-thousand rupee loan on a five hundred pound insurance policy, eighty pounds paid in premiums. He would recognise you, but you would have some trouble in recognising him.

Yet another was Michele D'Cruze, who, for love of Miss Vezzios, the nurse-girl, "black as a boot and, to our standard of taste, hideously ugly", managed to summon up enough courage to disperse the mob at Tibasu, where he was a telegraph-operator. Then there was the baby "who turned round in his father's arms, and said gravely, 'It is true that my name is Muhammad Din, *Tahib*, but I am not a *bubmash*, I am a man!'"

It must have been exhilarating to see so many different aspects of life and to be able to find the words for describing them. The tone of these stories must, however, have been extremely irritating to many critics who had no means then of telling what their author would grow into. He had about him, in prose as in verse, an infernally cynical knowingness. The author of *Certain Maxims of Hafiz* could be equally oracular as a story-teller. Racily and pithily expressed generalisations were there also a part of his method, and

Rudyard Kipling

few writers of his years can ever have had as much advice to give on the practical affairs of life. Scattered about *Plain Tales* alone there is all the wisdom of the smoking-room as it might have been epitomised by a greybeard.

For example:

Let a puppy eat the soap in the bath-room or chew a newly-blacked boot. He chews and chuckles until, by and by, he finds out that blacking and Old Brown Windsor make him very sick; so he argues that soap and boots are not wholesome. Any old dog about the house will soon show him the unwisdom of biting big dogs' ears. Being young, he remembers and goes abroad, at six months, a well-mannered little beast with a chastened appetite. If he had been kept away from boots, and soap, and big dogs till he came to the trinity full grown and with developed teeth, consider how fearfully sick and thrashed he would be! Apply that notion to the "sheltered life" and see how it works. It does not sound pretty, but it is the better of two evils.

Never praise a sister to a sister, in the hope of your compliments reaching the proper ears, and so preparing the way for you later on. Sisters are women first, and sisters afterwards; and you will find that you do yourself harm.

Racing leads to the *shroff* quicker than anything else. But if you have no conscience and no senti-

The Preparation

ments, and good hands, and some knowledge of pace, and ten years' experience of horses, and several thousand rupees a month, I believe that you can occasionally contrive to pay your shoeing-bills.

This drawling and cynical knowledge of the world comes from the mouth of a young man who had barely attained his majority. How some, or most, of it reached him he has revealed in one of the stories in *Soldiers Three*, where Mulvaney describes the rejection of his advances by Annie Bargin:

"Wid that I dropped my arm, fell back tu paces an' saluted, for I saw that she mint fhwat she said."

"Then you know something that some men would give a good deal to be certain of. How could you tell?" I demanded in the interests of Science.

"Watch the hand," said Mulvaney; "av she shuts her hand tight, thumb down over the knuckle, take up your hat an' go. You'll only make a fool av yourself av you shtay. But, av the hand lies opin on the lap, or av you see her thryin' to shut ut, an' she can't, — go on! She's not past reasonin' wid."

But to say that Kipling became worldly-wise by listening to the conversation of older and more experienced men does not carry us much further. Of course he did: he has told us so again and again. But it is one thing to seek for wisdom

Rudyard Kipling

from other mouths and another to recognise it when one hears it — and yet another to express it with the gnomic conciseness in which he excelled. Yet, whatever may be said in praise of Kipling's knowingness, it is not really an endearing quality, even if it is one that attracts the eye. It is impossible not to pay attention to the author of the pronouncements which I have quoted. But it is possible to find in the philosophy which they exemplify a little too much slickness and assurance, a tone, as it were, of brass. If Kipling had left us no more than the work of his Indian period, that would have had to bulk large in our final judgement — though we should have been equally obliged to say at the same time that he had written both poems and stories in which there is not a hint of brassiness.

Next we come to the charge which usually goes with those of vulgarity and cynicism, that of sentimentality. And this, too, has to be admitted. The best that can be said is that the young author, when he determines to be sentimental, does it in style and with skill. When the doctor says that there is a fair chance that Mrs. Gadsby may recover, Captain Gadsby, with his head on the neck of Mafflin's charger, exclaims, "Jack! I bub-bub-believe I'm going to make a bub-bub-bloody exhibition of myself", and Cap-

The Preparation

tain Mafflin, "sniffing openly and feeling in his left cuff", replies, "I-b-b — I'b doing it already. Old bad, what *cad* I say? I-b as pleased as — God *dab* you, Gaddy! You're one big idiot and I'b adother." Nothing particularly affecting, perhaps, in that inarticulate exchange, but, set where it is in the story, it is the little flick of the whip applied at the right moment to a raw place, that raw place having been carefully prepared beforehand by the author.

There are also stories of the type of *Only a Subaltern*. In this Bobby Wick works at his job, he earns the commendation of all those whose commendation really matters, he does the work of ten men in nursing the battalion through cholera, sustained only by letters from a girl whose spelling is touchingly faulty. When he received one of these his eyes "softened marvellously, and he was wont to fall into a tender abstraction for a while ere, shaking his cropped head, he charged into his work".

Throughout this story, Kipling, though in a sense he has made everything easy for himself, works with a sort of uneasy excess of effort. There is a private, whom Bobby Wicks has befriended, who says, on his death, "Orf'cer? — Bloomin' orf'cer? I'll learn you to misname the likes of 'im. Hangel! Bloomin' Hangel! that's

Rudyard Kipling

wot 'e is!" That, I think, is bad. We have something better in the behaviour of Bobby's company-commander:

Revere, his eyes red at the rims and his nose very white, went into Bobby's tent to write a letter to Papa Wick which should bow the white head of the ex-Commissioner of Chota-Buldana in the keenest sorrow of his life. Bobby's little store of papers lay in confusion on the table, and among them a half-finished letter. The last sentence ran: "So you see, darling, there is really no fear, because as long as I know you care for me and I care for you, nothing can touch me."

Revere stayed in the tent for an hour. When he came out his eyes were redder than ever.

There is nothing much in that, perhaps, except for the fact that Revere's nose turned white. There you have the Kipling who noticed things like that. He did probably learn from Browning — if not, I do not know where he can have learnt it — the trick of the apparently irrelevant detail which makes all the picture real. Here at the last moment it pulls the story back out of the unreality into which it has drifted. But, when a man is accused of being sentimental, to say that he is effectively sentimental is only to aggravate the offence. We will say that Kipling squeezed

The Preparation

out of his subject the last exacerbating drop it contained. He is a young giant who does not quite know his own strength.

Instances of this kind of excess, indeed, are to be found up and down all the work of the early Kipling, and it would be unfair to omit from this survey one instance which was published in a later collection. *Love-o'-Women* must be quoted because it shows better than any other story the faults of which the precociously brilliant author had to rid himself.

It belongs to the early days because it is placed in the mouth of Private Mulvaney, with prologue and epilogue by Private Ortheris. It is also one of the worst things that Kipling ever did, brilliant as are some of its descriptive passages. Larry, "Love-o'-Women", is thus described by his friend, Mulvaney:

I'm thinkin' he was suckled by a she-devil, for he never let wan go that came nigh to listen to him. 'Twas his business, as if it might ha' been sinthry-go. . . . 'Twas the nature av the baste to put the comether on the best av thim — not the prettiest by any manner av manes — but the like av such women as you cud lay your hand on the Book an' swear there was niver thought av foolishness in. An' for that very reason, mark you, he was niver caught.

Rudyard Kipling

But Larry's end, so harrowingly described, is simply the result of an infection that might as easily have befallen, say, three out of the five of the characters whom Kipling chastises but mildly for the follies of their youth. The moral drawn from it all is wholly false:

"But fwhat ails him, docthor?" I sez.

"They call it Locomotus attacks us," he sez, "bekaze," sez he, "ut attacks us like a locomotive, if ye know fwhat that manes. An' ut comes," sez he, lookin' at me, "ut comes from bein' called Love-o'-Women."

As everybody knows, it does not. Indeed, a man going Larry's black and wicked way runs rather less risk of such a death than do persons rather more innocent and rather more careless. The final scene on the verandah is sentimentality of really the worst sort, sentimentality masquerading as genuine passion, raw and biting as unmatured spirit.

"The house is open day an' night," she sez, wid a laugh; an' Love-o'-Women ducked his head an' hild up his hand as tho' he was gyardin'. The Power was on him still — it hild him up still, for, by my sowl, as I'll never save ut, he walked up the verandah steps that had been a livin' corpse in hospital for a month!

"An' now?" she sez, lookin' at him; an' the red

The Preparation

paint stud lone on the white av her face like a bull's-eye on a target.

He lifted up his eyes, slow an' very slow, an' he looked at her long an' very long, an' he tuk his spache betune his teeth wid a wrench that shuk him.

"I'm dyin', Aigypt — dyin'," he sez.

The best that can be said is that when Kipling descends to this sort of cheap theatricality he does it with a will. It is not a question of painting with a palette-knife instead of a brush; it is painting with a spade.

Yet a study of this story from the technical point of view helps us to estimate the enormous skill which he brought, even thus early, to his work. It *must* have been enormous, since not otherwise could the story have been even tolerable. *Love-o'-Women* is set most ingeniously inside the story of a shooting in barracks. Mulvaney says that the lucky man in that affair is the seducer who has been shot by the injured husband, and he tells the story proper to point that moral.

The whole piece begins with one of those introductory sentences of which Kipling has so marvellous a mastery: "The horror, the confusion and the separation of the murderer from his comrades were all over before I came". It goes on with a passage as magnificent in its com-

Rudyard Kipling

bination of exactness and evocativeness as any Kipling ever wrote:

There remained only on the barrack-square the blood of man calling from the ground. The hot sun had dried it to a dusky goldbeater-skin film, cracked lozenge-wise by the heat; and as the wind rose, each lozenge, rising a little, curled up at the edges as if it were a dumb tongue. Then a heavier gust blew all away down wind in grains of dark-coloured dust. It was too hot to stand in the sunshine before breakfast. The men were in barracks talking the matter over. A knot of soldiers' wives stood by one of the entrances to the married quarters, while inside a woman shrieked and raved with wicked filthy words.

It ends in the twilight with the guard and the witnesses from the trial going off, "marching easy and whistling". At the beginning and at the end, and all the way through, Kipling uses every conceivable device to subjugate the mind and, after that, the emotions of the reader. There are not many, if any, of his stories in which his resources as an artist are more extensively employed or displayed with as bold a strength and certainly none in which they are used for a less praiseworthy purpose.

It is now perhaps easy to understand the feelings of those to whom these stories came in quick succession at the end of the 'Eighties. It was im-

The Preparation

possible to ignore Kipling or even entirely to ignore him. But it was possible, natural indeed, to feel some uneasiness about him. He was new. He had discovered the riches of a New World: he was a sort of Cortez of literature. Or perhaps a better comparison would be with Clive. Clive returned home with wealth gained in India which earned him the reputation of being the richest man in England. No one knew how he was going to use it: most suspected that he would use it in a disturbing way. There were times when he seemed distressingly out of touch with what was considered proper in England. So with Kipling. He had all this treasure at his disposal. Did he mean to use it for the purpose of creating a disturbance? He was, above all, a new and unknown quantity.

His style, to be sure, was not entirely new. He owed obvious debts to earlier writers of the short story — to Poe (though his direct indebtedness is fully apparent in only one short story, *The Phantom Rickshaw*), to Maupassant, to Stevenson and, perhaps more than to anyone else, to Bret Harte. He owed as much again in a more general way to other teachers — especially to Browning, Swinburne and the Authorised Version of the Bible. But of that he never made any secret. He was always openly one of the most literary of

Rudyard Kipling

authors. He was willing to learn the tricks of his trade from anyone who could impart them to him. He zealously acknowledged his discipleships. To some of his favourite preceptors he paid the characteristic compliment of describing them as the objects of esoteric cults. He did this, for example, for Jane Austen, for the Stevenson of *The Wrong Box*, and for the creator of Brer Rabbit.

It did not matter, however, where the ingredients came from. The result was not to be described by any other name than that of Kipling and it was indisputably, disturbingly unfamiliar. The strange matter of these stories, from a territory hitherto almost untouched by literature, was conveyed in a style unlike any to which the English reading public had been accustomed. It was vivid in the last degree — sometimes, when the author judged it necessary, brutally vivid. Generally it was, to an almost sinister degree, brief and reticent in tone:

> Biel came out of the Court, and Strickland dropped a gut trainer's-whip in the verandah. Ten minutes later Biel was cutting Bronckhorst into ribbons behind the old Court cells, quietly and without scandal. What was left of Bronckhorst was sent home in a carriage; and his wife wept over it and nursed it into a man again.

The Preparation

This was indeed one of Kipling's most devastating tricks, to describe violent or horrible things "quietly and without scandal". Take, for an example, his story about "the Great Pop Picnic", in the course of which a man, bewildered by a dust-storm, makes his proposal to the wrong sister of two who are both in love with him. The error is ruthlessly rectified, and the narrator rides home with the girl to whom the first proposal has been mistakenly made. "Maud Copleigh," he says, "did not talk to me at any length." It is all done with this sort of drawling laconism, which makes the author's omniscience so much more effective and sometimes, no doubt, so much more exacerbating. The author, too, had a maddening talent for the invention of phrases and he set all England saying, "But that's another story" — which was, by the way, characteristic in its perfectly true suggestion that he had an almost inexhaustible store of stories to tell.

His prose style had, in short, all the qualities necessary for catching and holding attention. It varied within wide limits without ever ceasing to be individual and recognisable. It commanded a large and sometimes unexpected vocabulary. It seemed, as we shall presently see, to be the ideal medium for a doctrine for which the English-speaking world was fast growing ripe.

Rudyard Kipling

There was, however, another side to the wielder of these formidable powers which could not be overlooked. He seemed to be a great man in respect of the novelty of his material, of the novelty of his treatment of it, of the novelty of the ideas which he presented. He was great as a cultural phenomenon, if in no other way. But there was in fact another way — the way of sheer artistic achievement.

It is a favourite amusement among Kipling's admirers to make out lists of his best ten or fifteen or two dozen short stories. I have seen many such lists and have drawn up some of them myself. They vary a great deal — sometimes surprisingly — but I have never seen one which did not include *The Man Who Would Be King*. To this tale, which he wrote while he was still in India, Kipling gave all the virtuosity which he lavished on *Love-o'-Women*, without any danger of being betrayed by his material. Its fifty-two pages have enough packed in them to make the fortunes of a dozen romantic novels — and indeed several dozen romantic novels have been made out of fragments filched from these pages here and there. They are, to regard them from no other point of view, a miracle of compression. There is the distant beginning, the meeting between the

The Preparation

narrator and an odd wanderer in an "Intermediate" railway-carriage. Then comes the narrator's willingly accepted task of meeting a train as it crosses the Indian Desert and saying to a red-bearded man in a second-class carriage, "He has gone South for a week". Then the appearance of the preposterous two, Dravot and Carnehan, in the newspaper office with their preposterous "Contrack" and their preposterous plan for making themselves Kings, and their demand for maps which will show them the way into Kafiristan. Lastly, the reappearance of Carnehan, an insane scarecrow, with his account of how they did make themselves Kings and might have continued to be Kings had not Dravot departed from the "Contrack" in the article relating to women. Here a deeper note sounds than the brilliant but always self-conscious drawl of work that was in fact very little earlier:

He fumbled in the mass of rags round his bent waist; brought out a black horsehair bag embroidered with silver thread, and shook therefrom on to my table — the dried, withered head of Daniel Dravot! The morning sun that had long been paling the lamps struck the red beard and blind sunken eyes; struck, too, a heavy circlet of gold studded with raw turquoises, that Carnehan placed tenderly on the battered temples.
"You be'old now," said Carnehan, "the Emperor in his 'abit as he lived — the King of Kafiristan with his

Rudyard Kipling

crown upon his head. Poor old Daniel that was a monarch once!"

Justly might Mr. Wells's character describe this as "one of the best stories in the world". It is simply that, and no amount of analysis is likely to produce any more adequate description of it. It is a story perfectly told, with all its elements perfectly combined. And it was with this and other things in his pocket, and the certainty that he could do more as good and better, that the young man of twenty-four left India for the second and last time. He had long been anxious to go. Much as he loved journalism, he did not love being tied by service on the staff of a newspaper. Nor did he love the climate or the physical conditions of his work. Besides, there was all the rest of the world to see and understand and describe.

CHAPTER III

The Prophet of Empire

IT SOUNDS perhaps an odd thing to say at this point, but it is nevertheless true that when he left India Kipling's experience was relatively limited. He knew England as a schoolboy knows it, he had known India as a young child and now again as a young journalist. He had also made with his father that marvellous expedition to Paris. But that was all, and for a man so avid of knowledge it was not enough. In any case those seven years of hard work and development in India must have raised a formidable barrier between the man of twenty-four and the schoolboy on whose recollections he had to rely. Now the time had come for him to extend his acquaintanceship with the rest of the world. His position was secure, and there was no doubt as to the course

Rudyard Kipling

his career would follow. So he set out on his travels, fortified by a commission to describe them for the benefit of the readers of the Allahabad *Pioneer*. The results of that journey, with some other matter, are collected in the two volumes called *From Sea to Sea*.

The journey began with Burma and went thence to Hong Kong and Japan. After that Kipling crossed the Pacific to San Francisco and the American continent to pay a visit to a much revered author. The account of his interview with Mark Twain closes the record of this pilgrimage.

The book is not, I think, very much read today, and there is no great reason why it should be. Most of what was novel in it when it was written is less novel now. Moreover it becomes apparent that the style of Kipling's stories was a highly wrought and studied thing, and at this time was reserved for them alone. Here, writing impressions of travel for a newspaper, he is more diffuse, less exact and telling in his diction.

I do not mean that the book has no excellent things in it: there are many. High among them comes the tale of the "affable stranger of prepossessing appearance with a blue and innocent eye" who offered to show the traveller how life was lived in San Fransisco. Kipling accepted the offer and:

The Prophet of Empire

We arrived, always by the purest of chances, at a place where we could play cards, and also frivol with the Louisiana State Lottery tickets. Would I play? "Nay," said I, "for to me cards have neither meaning nor continuity; but let us assume that I am going to play. How would you and your friends get to work? Would you play a straight game, or make me drunk, or — well, the fact is I'm a newspaper man, and I'd be much obliged if you'd let me know something about bunco-steering."

The episode is characteristic, not least in the fact that, when he had finished cursing, the "bunco-steerer" did very amiably communicate to the enquirer some of the secrets of his profession. The same note is sounded again in another and a grimmer story, this time of the Chinese quarter of San Francisco which Kipling had rashly visited alone. There was a dispute between a Mexican and a Chinaman and the Chinaman reached for the other's winnings.

Mark how purely man is a creature of instinct. Rarely introduced to the pistol, I saw the Mexican half rise in his chair and at the same instant found myself full length on the floor. None had told me that this was the best attitude when bullets are abroad. I was there prone before I had time to think — dropping as the room was filled with an intolerable clamour like the discharge of a cannon. In those close quarters the

Rudyard Kipling

pistol report had no room to spread any more than the smoke — then acrid in my nostrils. There was no second shot, but a great silence in which I rose slowly to my knees. The Chinaman was gripping the table with both hands and staring in front of him at an empty chair. The Mexican had gone, and a little whirl of smoke was floating near the roof. Still gripping the table, the Chinaman said: "Ah!" in the tone that a man would use when, looking up from his work suddenly, he sees a well-known friend in the doorway. Then he coughed and fell over to his own right, and I saw that he had been shot in the stomach.

I doubt whether Kipling would ever have passed this in a story or, in his later years, in anything else. But it is, all the same, fine descriptive reporting.

But what is most interesting today in *From Sea to Sea* is the light which it throws on the formation of Kipling's political ideas — and on the extent to which they were already formed when he left India. These ideas will form the subject of the present chapter, and in my endeavour to elucidate them I shall have to go far ahead of my account of his work as an artist. That, however, will present but small inconvenience, since, once the ideas were formed, they changed little. The only major change was in his attitude towards the creed he made out of the implications he found in them.

The Prophet of Empire

Japan, the first country he visited outside the sphere of British rule, was indeed a test-case for him. Here was an Eastern nation which was hard at work in the adoption of Western civilisation of its own free will and by its own efforts. This was a different situation from that obtaining in India, and the two cried out to be set beside one another for comparison.

When Kipling arrived in Tokio, he ought, he says, to have done several things, including making calls on the leaders of the political parties. But he heard bugles and went to look at the Japanese army instead. He found the infantry largely good, reminding him of the Gurkhas. He thought less highly of the cavalry. All the officers filled him with contempt, and he thought that to make out of the Japanese troops material as good as they might be British officers should be employed.[1] He makes one incidental comment which is worth remembering:

> The worst of conscription is that it sweeps in such a mass of fourth- and fifth-rate citizens who, though they may carry a gun, are likely by their own excusable ineptitude, to do harm to the morale and set-up of a regiment.

[1] Foreign military observers in China recently seem to have been unanimously of the opinion that three Japanese divisions might be a match for one European division.

Rudyard Kipling

On the state of politics in Japan he is quite uncompromising. "Japan," he says, "is the second Oriental country which has made it impossible for a strong man to govern alone. This she has done of her own free will. India, on the other hand, has been forcibly ravished by the Secretary of State and the English M.P." The new Japanese Constitution had been published just before his arrival and wherever he went he was asked whether he had read it. He was dubious about the benefits it would confer and argued with his hosts:

"We shall be happy with this Constitution and a people civilised among civilisations!"

"Of course. But what will you actually do with it? A Constitution is rather a monotonous thing to work after the fun of sending members to Parliament has died out. You have a Parliament, have you not?"

"Oh, yes, *with* parties – Liberal and Radical."

"Then they will both tell lies to you and to each other. Then they will pass bills, and spend their time fighting each other. Then all the foreign governments will discover that you have no fixed policy."

He was hardened in these opinions, if that were needed, which is perhaps doubtful, by what he saw and heard in America. Here is his summary of American politics:

Turn now to the august spectacle of a Government of the people, by the people, for the people, as it is

The Prophet of Empire

understood in the city of San Francisco. Professor Bryce's book will tell you that every American citizen over twenty-one years of age possesses a vote. He may not know how to run his own business, control his wife, or instil reverence into his children, may be pauper, half-crazed with drink, bankrupt, dissolute, or merely a born fool; but he has a vote. If he likes, he can be voting most of his time — voting for his State Governor, his municipal officers, local option, sewage contracts, or anything else of which he has no special knowledge.

The young man who had had a pretty close view of the Government of India, as an object-lesson in political science, and who had formed these opinions on his travels returned to an England where a number of things had happened since as a schoolboy he had last left her. Notable among them were the defeat at Majuba, with the subsequent surrender to the Boers, and the abandonment of General Gordon at Khartoum. There had been also the whole of the Irish business, outrages in Ireland herself and obstruction in the House of Commons and Gladstone's attempt to establish Home Rule. To many it seemed that the British Empire had entered upon a period of weakness and decay, which if it were not checked, must end in ruin. Now here was a writer who had already brought himself into notice by offering

Rudyard Kipling

to the public fascinating novelties of both style and subject, and who knew the Empire, or an important part of it, at first hand. He was prepared to issue the same warning and to back it with arguments and concrete illustrations. He came very much at the opportune moment, and it is hardly surprising that, in his twenties, he enjoyed a position given before only to Dickens and Tennyson among English writers — a position equal, almost, to theirs in degree and strikingly different from theirs in kind.

There is some reflection of the success he enjoyed in Dick Heldar's exclamation in *The Light That Failed:* "I like the power; I like the fun; I like the fuss; and above all I like the money. I almost like the people who make the fuss and pay the money." But Dick's success in the novel was no more than a shadow of Kipling's in reality during the magic decade between his return to England and the beginning of the South African War. When he died, it was amusing to see the unanimity with which every newspaper remembered that, during his serious illness in 1899, the German Emperor made telegraphic enquiries about his health. But the unanimity was not so naive as it might seem. The German Emperor was probably not aware of the merits of Rudyard Kipling as a literary artist, though one of his subjects produced, at the low

The Prophet of Empire

price of threepence, a translation of a work called *Schlichte Geschichten aus den Hügeln*. But he did know when he was in the presence of an historical fact. An historical fact is what Rudyard Kipling made himself at this time and, while we consider him apart from his literary excellence, it is as a fact that we must consider him. England had long been under the spell of Gladstonian Liberalism. She was ripe for a change. Kipling had the match to set the fire going. He did at any rate help to set it going. That is all that need be said of his public importance up to this point. But, the state of world affairs being what it was, it was enough to justify the attention paid to him by a foreign monarch.

Throughout this curious time, his own behaviour was remarkable. I am speaking of his public behaviour, which was remarkable because there was none of it. In the most astonishing way he refused to be lionised either now or hereafter. I think it can be taken as certain that he regarded himself as a man with a mission, with a gospel to preach. Nothing must be allowed to interfere with that mission, and therefore he ate very austerely of the fruits of his success.

Beresford's reminiscences have recently revived the old story that he would have liked to be Poet Laureate, and missed the appointment only be-

Rudyard Kipling

cause of the inflexible opposition of Queen Victoria, who had never liked being called "the Widder o' Windsor". General Dunsterville, who is in as good a position to judge, doubts the story. He says, "I believe that Kipling never had a hankering after that high honour, which would hamper the freedom of his muse". This is putting it in the wrong way. The Laureateship did not hamper Wordsworth or Tennyson or Bridges and seems so far to have left Mr. Masefield's Muse reasonably untrammelled. If Kipling had been only a poet, there could have been no reason why he should not have aspired to the place. But, as I have said, it is a matter of common knowledge that, at one time or another, he might have had every honour which it is in the power of a British Government to bestow. He accepted none of them, and the reason — common knowledge again — was that he would not accept a gift from a Government which he might afterwards find himself obliged to attack. (There was in this something of the sage resolution of the schoolboy poet who did not show to his friends the exciting volume which his father had had printed for him.) It is possible, it is easy, to disagree with his political views. It would be very hard indeed to show, or even to suggest, that he ever held or expressed them for his own personal advantage.

The Prophet of Empire

A part, even a large part, but still only a part, of his doctrine is summarised in such phrases as "the white man's burden". He was an Imperialist. He belonged to the generation in which that word began to take shape and active meaning. While he was still at the United Services College (and not long before he wrote *Ave Imperatrix*) Cecil Rhodes was drawing up that one of his many wills in which he bequeathed the bulk of his still unmade fortune for the foundation of a secret society which was to establish Anglo-Saxon domination over the whole world.

I do not know, it would probably, in spite of *Ave Imperatrix*, be very hard to discover, what political ideas Kipling had in his head when he went to India. There is no question as to the ideas he brought back with him. From that system in its main lines he never departed. But since it is expressed almost entirely in a series of imaginative compositions, it is open to interpretation in several different ways. And there are some expressions of it which have proved stumbling-blocks even to the most devoted of his admirers. Here is one which has often been quoted against him:

Now remember when you're 'acking round a gilded
    Burma god
  That 'is eyes is very often precious stones;
An' if you treat a nigger to a dose o' cleanin'-rod

Rudyard Kipling

'E's like to show you everything 'e owns.
When 'e won't prodooce no more, pour some water on
    the floor
    Where you 'ear it answer 'ollow to the boot
              (*Cornet:* Toot! toot!)
When the ground begins to sink, shove your baynick
    down the chink,
    An' you're sure to touch the ——
(*Chorus*) Loo! loo! Lulu! Loot! loot! loot!
        Ow the loot!

This is wholly detestable, and it makes the commentator on Kipling turn red when he endeavours to explain it. The best that can be said is that certain difficulties are likely to arise when the exposition of a political philosophy is in the hands of what Flecker called "a thought-breathing poet". The poet, contemplating the whole system and finding it pretty good, is apt to be carried away in a mood of misplaced enthusiasm by the exciting picturesqueness of some of its defects. The imposition of discipline and the use of military force, which Kipling sees as means to a good end, involve some risk of slips on the part of the human instrument. It is a thousand pities he did not say so. This poem in all probability has done his reputation more harm than anything else he ever wrote.

But, taking his work as a whole, it is unfair to represent him as applauding violence and rapine

The Prophet of Empire

for their own sake. This is perhaps the place to examine his preoccupation with war and things military. Let it be admitted at the outset that, up to a certain point, war may be a good game. It does call out many admirable qualities, and innumerable philosophers before Kipling (Ruskin, for example, who was not physically a very warlike man) have argued that on balance these outweigh the suffering it causes. We do sometimes display now what Matthew Arnold detected in the other occupants of his first-class carriage, an almost bloodthirsty clinging to life. There is, moreover, something of weight in the insistence of such thinkers as Mr. Wells and Mr. Olaf Stapledon on the fact that danger is a necessary element in the well-adjusted life. Nowadays the dangers brought by war not only to the individual but also to the whole of civilisation outweigh its attractions. And there are other preferable dangers which can be courted in the search for the well-adjusted life. You can crash while testing a new type of aeroplane, or you can drown, like Gino Watkins, in the Greenland seas, or freeze, like Irvine and Mallory, on the top of Everest.

When Kipling first began to form his philosophy, war was still only one of these dangers, no more excessive than the others, and, in his view, as likely as they to justify itself by good results

Rudyard Kipling

for humanity in general. He thought that the inhabitants of India had benefited by British rule, and British rule over them had been established by war, and readiness for war to defend them, who could not defend themselves, against potential other rulers who would not do so much for them as the British had done.

The idea of war as a game was never far absent from Kipling's mind and he often urged it, especially in *The Army of a Dream*. But, before most of us had realised how different from a game of reasonable risks it had become, he was looking forward to a time when it would be thought to be an anachronism. There are, he was ready to say, other risks which will equally satisfy the same healthy appetite. But in the 'Eighties and 'Nineties war did seem to him to be one of the necessary instruments of good government.

Good government was the essence of the doctrine he preached, and he thought it might be attained by the principle of what, in the modern jargon, is called "Hierarchy". He criticised the English people and many of their institutions bitterly enough, but he did believe that they threw up, in greater numbers than any other people, men who are entitled to be called rulers. It would be easy to call him as a witness against the whole fabric of British rule in India. He provided texts

The Prophet of Empire

in profusion throughout his Indian years. *The Masque of Plenty* records how the Government of India sent out a commission to enquire into economic conditions. It is a long and very lively poem, from which only two quotations need be made. The first is:

HIRED BAND, *brasses only, full chorus* —
    God bless the Squire
    And all his rich relations
    Who teach us poor people
    We eat our proper rations —
    We eat our proper rations,
    In spite of inundations,
    Malarial exhalations,
    And casual starvations,
We have, we have, they say we have —
We *have* our proper rations.

The second is from the concluding "Chorus of the Crystallised Facts", about "The Much Administered Man":

    In the towns of the North and the East,
    They gathered as unto rule,
    They bade him starve his priest
    And send his children to school.
    Railways and roads they wrought,
    For the needs of the soil within;
    A time to squabble in court,
    A time to bear and to grin.

Rudyard Kipling

And gave him peace in his ways,
Jails — and Police to fight,
Justice — at length of days,
And Right — and Might in the Right.
His speech is of mortgaged bedding,
On his kine he borrows yet,
At his heart is his daughter's wedding,
In his eyes foreknowledge of debt.
He eats and hath indigestion,
He toils and he may not stop;
His life is a long-drawn question
Between a crop and a crop.

Kipling's case, however, was that, though there was still almost everything for the British to do in India, yet they had done more than any of her other rulers in the past and more than anyone else was likely to do in the future.

But it was indispensable that they should be allowed to rule, that they should be recognised as a ruling race. In *His Chance in Life*, we are told never to forget that "unless the outward and visible signs of Our Authority are always before a native he is as incapable as a child of understanding what authority is or where is the danger of disobeying it". It is in this story that Michele D'Cruze, one-eighth white, becomes a ruler for the moment because:

The Prophet of Empire

The Police Inspector, afraid, but obeying the old instinct which recognises a drop of white blood as far as it can be diluted, said, "What orders does the *Sahib* give?"

The "*Sahib*" decided Michele. Though horribly frightened, he felt that, for the hour, he, the man with the Cochin Jew and the menial uncle in his pedigree, was the only representative of English authority in the place.

There is a more poignant instance in the scene in *Kim* in which the boy who has lived most of his life without knowing that he is a white man is made to assert his authority as a Sahib over his departmental chief, the Bengali Hurree Chunder Mookerjee, who has cherished, trained and castigated him. Kim is reluctant, but knows that his blood imposes on him a duty which he must not shirk, and the Babu willingly acquiesces. The example is the more significant in that there are few of his characters for whom Kipling shows a more obvious admiration than Hurree Chunder Mookerjee. But there is a principle to be maintained which overrides all individual exceptions. The relation of the Babu to Kim *is because it must be*, because that is the way in which things can best be made to work, the same as that of Baloo the bear and Bagheera the panther towards Mowgli. The two animals are older and wiser but Mowgli is a man.

Rudyard Kipling

How far Kipling regards this as inevitable, and, what is still more important, unchangeable, is not so easy to decide. It is easier than is quite safe to make deductions from one story or even from two or three. In *The Head of the District* he makes a merciless attack on the Viceroy who decided to make an "appointment, always on principle, of a man of the people to rule the people". The practical application of this principle meant the promotion of Mr. Grish Chunder Dé, M.A., from a district in South-eastern Bengal to a Deputy Commissionership in a less tranquil neighbourhood where "the cultivators were not gentle people, the miners for salt were less gentle still, and the cattle-breeders were least gentle of all". There were, besides, the Khosru-Kheyl across the border. When the Khosru-Kheyl broke loose it was bad for Grish Chunder Dé, who fled from a task which was impossible for him. Bloody disorder ensued, and it was put right only by the leadership of white men.

But this does not necessarily mean that Kipling condemns all Indian natives as unfit to rule. Consider that beautiful story, *The Miracle of Purun Bhagat* — for other reasons than its beauty. Sir Purun Dass, K.C.I.E., the Prime Minister of a native state, is represented as being a discreet, firm,

The Prophet of Empire

tactful administrator, a man after his creator's own heart.

As we have seen, Kipling never argued that British rule in India was perfect. He has accused it of innumerable mistakes (such, for example, as the appointment of Mr. Grish Chunder Dé) made through ignorance of the people with whom it has to deal. There was, again, a gross misunderstanding of elementary facts in the Bill for the Sub-montane Tracts which was removed in time only because six-year-old Tods had both many friends in the bazaar and also the ear of a Legal Councillor. Kipling was, indeed, a severe and penetrating critic of the British regime. But he did think it, with all its imperfections, the best system that India ever has had or is likely to have for many years to come.

In a book belonging to a much later period he describes the work of regeneration done by the British in the Sudan:

> The men who remember the old days of the Reconstruction — which deserves an epic of its own — say that there was nothing left to build on, not even wreckage. Knowledge, decency, kinship, property, title, sense of possession had all gone. The people were told they were to sit still and obey orders; and they stared and fumbled like dazed crowds after an explosion. . . . And little by little, as they realised that the

Rudyard Kipling

new order was sure and that their ancient oppressors were quite dead, there returned not only cultivators, craftsmen, and artisans, but outlandish men of war, scarred with old wounds and the generous dimples that the Martini-Henry bullet used to deal — fighting men on the look-out for new employ.

Something like that the British did, over a longer space of years, in India, often helped in their work of establishing peace by "fighting men on the look-out for new employ". And of course the reconstruction of the Sudan, after the destruction of the Khalifa at Omdurman, could not have been carried out so swiftly or so efficiently without the help of a technique developed principally in India.

Technique and the technician are the pivots of Kipling's political thought. He was fundamentally and esentially an "authoritarian", and he had one immutable principle: "The job belongs to the man who can do it." In his earlier days, when it was still possible to regard war as a game, very dangerous perhaps, but still a game, he was inclined to attach too much importance to the military technique. But in his work as a whole the technique of those engaged in more peaceful, if not always safer, pursuits does receive more attention. There is a story of his praising Pierre Loti to a French visitor and then saying, "What sort of an officer is he? Professionally, I mean." Pre-

The Prophet of Empire

cisely so would he have enquired about a foreign author who happened to be known also a ploughman or an electrician.

Nothing ever interested him as much as the way in which men did their jobs. And, for that matter, animals. Rikki-Tikki-Tavi "knew that all a grown mongoose's business in life was to fight and eat snakes", and he did it extremely well, as his biographer takes joy in saying. It is the same wherever we look — fishermen on the Grand Bank, experts in seamanship, and in catching, cleaning and salting fish, or the contingent which fights the famine in *William the Conqueror*, or Dick Heldar making his sketches in *The Light that Failed*. The penultimate and, as I think, the richest period in Kipling's life and work began when he discovered at home the counterpart of what he had seen in so many strange places abroad — the age-old, elaborate and exquisite technique of the English countryman. The compendious expression of that discovery is to be found in the poem called *The Land:*

When Julius Fabricius, Sub-prefect of the Weald,
In the days of Diocletian owned our Lower Riverfield,
He called to him Hobdenius — a Briton of the Clay,
Saying: "What about that River-piece for layin' in to hay?"

Rudyard Kipling

And the aged Hobden answered: "I remember as a lad
My father told your father that she wanted dreenin' bad.
An' the more that you neeglect her the less you'll get her clean.
Have it jest *as* you've a mind to, but if I was you I'd dreen."

. . . . .

"Hob, what about that River-bit?" I turn to him again
With Fabricius and Ogier and William of Warenne.
"Hev it jest as you've a mind to, *but*" — and so he takes command.
For whoever pays the taxes old Mus' Hobden owns the land.

This is a very good exemplification of the principle that "the job belongs to the man who can do it". But the supreme exemplification is in the job of ruling. It is because of this that Kipling is an authoritarian. He never departed from the opinion which he brought away with him from India and which made him lament that "Japan is the second Oriental country which has made it impossible for a strong man to govern alone". The machinery of a strong government affects him with the same rapturous awe as, say, the machinery of a well-designed locomotive:

The Prophet of Empire

Mrs. Hauksbee began reading. I have said the batch was rather important. That is quite enough for you to know. It referred to some correspondence, two measures, a peremptory order to a native chief, and two dozen other things. Mrs. Hauksbee gasped as she read, for the first glimpse of the naked machinery of the Great Indian Government, stripped of its casings, and lacquer, and paint, and guard-rails, impresses the most stupid man.

Such a machine as this, in his view, a democracy could never either fashion or handle. This was not a conviction which came to him in the hardening process of the years. It was early formed and, when once it had been formed, was not changed. Democracy meant to him simply a system under which incompetent people strove to take work out of the hands of people competent to do it. It appeared to him to be sheer wasteful and injurious inefficiency that electors and their representatives in England should legislate for India and for peoples and conditions of which they had not the smallest experience. By extension, it seemed to him absurd that they should attempt to govern themselves, when men were to be found with a special gift for government, just as other men are found with special gift for running marine engines or for working the land.

His sketch of an Utopia is contained in two

Rudyard Kipling

stories which I have already mentioned — *With the Night Mail* and *As Easy as A.B.C.* In the first of these he explains that the Aerial Board of Control:

That semi-elected, semi-nominated body of a few score persons of both sexes controls this planet. "Transportation is Civilisation", our motto runs. Theoretically we do what we please so long as we do not interfere with the traffic and *all it implies*. Practically, the A.B.C. confirms or annuls all international arrangements and, to judge from its last report, finds our tolerant, humorous, lazy little planet only too ready to shift the whole burden of public administration on to its shoulders.

The same story has as appendix a number of extracts from a newspaper of that future day, including one describing an important political event. Crete, it seems, had been "the sole surviving repository of 'autonomous institutions', 'local self-government', and the rest of the archaic lumber devised in the past for the confusion of human affairs". This brought her a good deal of tourist traffic. But at last the islanders tired of "playing at savages for pennies" and cut off all communications in order to force the A.B.C. to annex them, which it did.

There is further illumination in the second story which describes a world still shuddering

The Prophet of Empire

from its recollections of the horrors of democracy and apt to turn angry against those who advocate the revival of democratic practices. The inhabitants of Illinois are thus alarmed and get so much out of hand that the Board has to send the fleet to pacify them, which it does by means of painful lights and sounds. But first it hears them singing *Macdonough's Song*.

Once there was The People — Terror gave it birth,
Once there was The People and it made a Hell of
    Earth.
Earth arose and crushed it. Listen, O ye slain!
Once there was The People — it shall never be again!

Then the would-be democrats or "Serviles" are introduced to justify Kipling's opinion of them by their own words:

It appeared that our Planet lay sunk in slavery beneath the heel of the Aerial Board of Control. The orator urged us to arise in our might, burst our prison doors and break our fetters (all his metaphors, by the way, were of the most mediaeval). Next he demanded that every matter of daily life, including most of the physical functions, should be submitted for decision at any time of the week, month, or year to, I gathered, anybody who happened to be passing by or residing within a certain radius, and that everybody should forthwith abandon his concerns to settle the

Rudyard Kipling

matter, first by crowd-making, next by talking to the crowds made, and lastly by describing crosses on pieces of paper, which rubbish should later be counted with certain mystic ceremonies and oaths. Out of this amazing play, he assured us, would automatically arise a higher, nobler, and kinder world, based — he demonstrated this with the awful lucidity of the insane — based on the sanctity of the Crowd and the villainy of the single person.

These stories give us, as I have said, only a rough sketch of an Utopia. They argue about nothing. They leave a very great deal for the imagination to fill in at will. But, even so, the difficulty in Kipling's political system is immediately obvious. It lies in two words in the first of the preceding quotations. The Aerial Board of Control is "semi-elected, semi-nominated". But how and by whom, without some sort of democratic machinery, elected? And by whom nominated? The problem of Kipling's ideal world-state is simply the choice of its governors and it is a problem which, in these two stories at any rate, he does not attempt to solve. Presumably in practice those with an aptitude and taste for administration find themselves naturally in directing positions. We find that under the A.B.C. there is a Mayor of Chicago, with assistants, who include a Chief of Police. And the Mayor says an interesting thing:

The Prophet of Empire

"Then the Serviles turned in all tongue-switches and talked, and we ——"

"What did they talk about?" said Takahira.

"First, how badly things were managed in the city. That pleased us Four — we were on the platform — because we hoped to catch one or two good men for City work. You know how rare executive capacity is."

But are the self-selected, who owe their positions to the indifference of the governed, always efficient? Are they efficient enough even to keep the governed permanently indifferent? And do they always select themselves merely because they have a bent for administration? It can be argued that the less desirable results of democracy spring from an indifference among the governed which is quite extensive enough already. One finds it hard to believe that the same persons whom we now decry as "politicians" would fail to select themselves for public office when that indifference became complete.

My immediate business here, however, is not so much to criticise Kipling's ideas as, if I can, to set them forth. He certainly always had at the back of his mind an administrative organisation which served him as a model of the government to which he would have liked to entrust the world's affairs. He had seen the Indian Civil Service at

Rudyard Kipling

work and he had found it, not perfect to be sure, but in the main a corps of able, hard-working and disinterested men. It was, further, a corps with a long tradition of ability, industry, and disinterestedness. He believed that, under the leadership of "a strong man governing alone", it would be as good an administrative organisation as the world had ever known, at any rate since the best days of the Roman Empire. He believed that it could be adapted for use in other parts of the world. He preached the doctrine of Imperialism in the interests of good government.

No doubt in much that he said and felt there was an alloy of the unreasoning and superficial which can properly be called Jingoism. But the doctrine which he preached in the 'Nineties was neither unreasoning nor superficial. He believed in the British Empire precisely in the way in which Cecil Rhodes believed in it — as an engine of progress and of general happiness for the ordinary family. (There is, by the way, no narrow nationalism in his Utopia: the members of the Aerial Board of Control whom he names are De Forest, Dragomiroff, Takahira and Piroli.) Returning home with a gospel and with a platform of his own building whence to preach it, he endeavoured to arouse among the English that sense of a right to empire, derived strictly from

The Prophet of Empire

their fitness for it, which did not exist among the Romans when their empire was undergoing its widest expansion, but which was expressed by the Augustan poets. It was in a sense a literary derivation. But it came to Kipling at a remove. Before he began to interpret it in poetry, it had been re-translated into fact. The Augustan poets glorified the situation they found. The English administrators who had read them intensively at school took from them a code. To the Englishman in India *parcere subjectis et debellare superbos* was something that he took as seriously as honouring his father and his mother. Kipling made poetry out of something which had its origins in poetry. But he was concerned with what he could see under his own eyes, not with its origins. At school he hated the classics. It was only in much later years that Horace became one of his favourite authors. (Virgil, by the way, apparently never did.) He now saw the Roman author through a medium which made for comprehension.

When he first returned to England he was full of his gospel. Richard le Gallienne described very well the significance of this phase in his development. "In 1890," he said

we were saying to each other, with a sense of freemasonry in a new cult: "But that is another story." Today we are exhorting each other to: "Take up the

Rudyard Kipling

white man's burden." The value of each phrase is about the value of Mr. Kipling's reputation in 1890 and 1899, respectively. The smart young Anglo-Indian story-teller is now a prophet. His fame is a church.

In this phase he provided a voice for a considerable section of public opinion which was only waiting for such help to become vocal. But he did not necessarily take always the popular line. There is gross and demonstrable injustice in the suggestion that he gained popularity by flattering the prejudices of the comfortable classes. It is true that he enabled soft stay-at-homes to rejoice in their superiority over "natives" whom they had never encountered. But he could hardly help that. He took his own line, regardless of those who might think themselves flattered or those who might think themselves insulted. For a good deal of the spirit on which he relied to make the perfect world of infallible administration he looked to the public school. But some aspects of "the public school spirit" so galled his patience that he wrote the famous and much disliked line about "flannelled fools at the wicket and muddied oafs at the goal". This was almost striking in the face the public which supported him. Then, in *Stalky & Co.*, he took his life as an author in his hands. It could not have been other than a violent shock

The Prophet of Empire

to readers brought up on *Tom Brown's Schooldays*. To publish these stories was a more daring thing than today we can easily realise. The venture succeeded because the stories were superb of their sort. He earned the right to speak by being a superb story-teller: he kept it by continuing to be a superb story-teller. But he was determined to speak.

At the height of his career as a prophet he was not concerned to endear himself to his own people by comfortable words. The height of it, as we can see better now than anyone could then, was the *Recessional*, which he wrote for Queen Victoria's Diamond Jubilee. It was a boastful and arrogant moment, and Kipling is often supposed to have been a boastful and arrogant writer. Indeed one phrase from this piece is sometimes quoted in support of that belief. The phrase is "lesser breeds without the Law". The sense of the phrase, however, is to be seen in the last three words and not in the first two. There is room for all within the Law, which sees no breed which has accepted it as greater or lesser than another. And the whole poem is an admonition to the English as to a people which must humbly keep the law as a special trust.

It is impossible here to avoid a discursive examination of the circumstances in which this

Rudyard Kipling

poem was written and published. There are three not wholly congruent accounts. Kipling's own, in *Something of Myself*, is not elaborate, but is very illuminating. He says that something in the spirit of self-confidence displayed by the English at the Diamond Jubilee scared him. He therefore wrote these lines as a "*nuzzur-wattu* (an averter of the Evil Eye)". Then he went off on naval manœuvres with a friend and, on his return, judged that the time was ripe for publication.

A more detailed story is printed by Mr. R. Thurston Hopkins, apparently in the poet's own words, though without any reference to the source where they are to be found:

"That poem gave me more trouble than anything I ever wrote. I had promised *The Times* a poem on the Jubilee, and when it became due I had written nothing that satisfied me. *The Times* began to want that poem badly, and sent letter after letter asking for it. I had many more attempts, but no further progress. Finally *The Times* began sending telegrams. So I shut myself in a room with the determination of remaining there until I had written a Jubilee poem.

"Sitting with all my previous attempts before me I searched through these dozens of sketches till at last I found just one line I liked. That was 'Lest we forget.' Round these words *Recessional* was written."

The Prophet of Empire

This might of course be reconciled, though not very satisfactorily, with Kipling's own version. So, I suppose, could some of the details in the third and latest version. Even this, however, would not be easy — the dates are utterly irreconcilable — and the third cannot in any way be made to agree with the second. But it has striking documentary evidence to support it.

It rests on the original MS. now in the British Museum and on the testimony of Miss Sara Norton, an American lady who was staying with the Kiplings at Rottingdean on July 16th, 1897 — about a month after Jubilee Day. Kipling was throwing papers into his waste-paper basket, from which Miss Norton retrieved one bearing a set of verses called *After*. She thought it ought to be published. Kipling still did not. After argument, it was decided to submit the question to his aunt, Lady Burne-Jones, who also was strongly in favour of publication. The poem was then and there revised, with marginal annotations, including a mention of the use of "Sallie's pen" and the MS. bears at its foot the note:

done in consultation at North End House. July 16.
    Aunt Georgie
    Sallie
    Carrie and me.

Rudyard Kipling

It was published in *The Times* of the following day. Presumably the fair copy must have been sent to London by train.

This would make a better problem in historical detection were it not so obvious that we shall never get much further than comparing likelihoods. Did the editor of *The Times* commission Kipling to write a poem on the Jubilee? He must have done if he got to the point of sending him telegrams about it. But, if he did, surely he would not have thought of a ceremonial piece to be delivered a month after the important occasion. There is nothing extraordinary in the incident of the family council. Kipling was always willing to accept any help he could get. There was not in his nature any of the egotism of the minor artist who insists that what bears his name must be solely his. He records with joy and pride that once, when he was worrying over an unsatisfactory but crucial line, his mother said: "You're *trying* to say, 'What do they know of England who only England know?'" There is no reason apparent why he should not tell us that an American guest rescued *Recessional* from the fire and that Aunt Georgie recommended him to publish it.

I suggest a plausible reason. There was something going on in his mind, a premonition, such

The Prophet of Empire

as often came to him, of a change in his attitude towards life which would take effect later. *Recessional* was for him a turning-point. No sooner had he written it than he began to realise that, without knowing it, at the back of his mind, he had begun to think in a different way about the mission of the British people. Well might he have hesitated to publish the poem. It probably surprised him when he considered its significance. Poets do sometimes learn for the first time what has been going on in their minds when they see the results of it on paper. I imagine that he assured himself that it meant nothing — that it was only the record of a passing mood. But the giving of it to the world would mean, for himself, even if the world did not (and it did not) understand what he was saying, going through a gate which opened only one way. I suggest that here we have the moment in which Kipling changed from a brilliant man into a great man.

II

Many things were to happen before the change worked itself out in all its potentialities. It was consummated by events the substance of which he had seen in the clairvoyance of a poet. We shall come to them later. At present we must pursue, beyond this moment of *Recessional*, the history of his political ideas.

Let us begin by asking what he meant by "the Law." It is the law of civilisation, of progress. He sometimes expresses his conception of it in terms which lend themselves to cultured jeering. He appears to deify the locomotive, the steamship, the motor-car, and these are, as we know, vulgar things mainly used to carry trippers to places where they make inept comments on the scenery and leave sandwich-wrappings in the hedgerows. But Kipling did not deify them for this reason, nor even simply because they were great and powerful. He exalted them because he saw in them instruments for conveying the first elements of happiness to mankind. He lived impressionable and formative years in a country where it can truly be said of the average man that:

> His life is a long-drawn question
> Between a crop and a crop.

He had seen, and he has described, what may happen when the answer to the question is a black one. There is, no doubt, much more to be said about the details of British rule in India than is said in *William the Conqueror*, but no one who knows anything about Indian history will deny the veracity of this picture of famine and its relief.

The Prophet of Empire

The relief workers were hurried to the scene of their work by railway:

Here the people crawled to the side of the train, holding their little ones in their arms; and a loaded truck would be left behind, men and women clustering round and above it like ants by spilled honey. Once in the twilight they saw on a dusty plain a regiment of little brown men, each bearing a body over his shoulder; and when the train stopped to leave yet another truck, they perceived that the burdens were not corpses, but only foodless folk picked up beside their dead oxen by a corps of irregular troops.

They lived in trains, supplies for the starving came in trains, and when it was all over the workers were taken in trains back to their proper jobs. Kipling disliked famines and to him "the Law" was something which, by means of its servants, modern machinery and devoted disinterested administrators, would in time eliminate them. During the decade 1901–11 the population of India increased by 19 per cent. and the increase was largely due to the fact that in the 'Eighties innumerable children had been saved from death by starvation. Whether India has really benefited from this increase in her population is another question, which different people will answer in different ways. But I do not suppose that many

Rudyard Kipling

will argue that famine is a good way of keeping the population at its optimum level.

For a light from a different angle on Kipling's conception of "the Law" we must go forward a little out of our period. I have already said once or twice that Rome was not absent from his mind. As his experience widened and his mind mellowed, the importance of the Roman example seemed to him ever greater. In *Puck of Pook's Hill,* written during the years between the South African War and the Great War, there are three stories which give as good an imaginative picture of Britain in the last century of Roman rule as any in existence. Parnesius comes of a Roman family long settled in the Isle of Wight. At the end of his boyhood he goes to Aquae Sulis:

The best baths in Britain. Just as good, I'm told, as Rome. All the old gluttons sit in hot water, and talk scandal and politics. And the Generals come through the streets with their guards behind them; and the magistrates come in their chairs with their stiff guards behind them; and you meet fortune-tellers, and gold-smiths, and merchants, and feather-sellers, and ultra-Roman Britons, and ultra-British Romans, and tame tribesmen pretending to be civilised, and Jew lecturers, and — oh, everybody interesting.

The Prophet of Empire

While there, he decides that he wants to be a soldier. Then we see him marching north in charge of a draft intended for the garrison of the Wall:

"The hard road goes on and on — and the wind sings through your helmet-plume — past altars to Legions and Generals forgotten, and broken statues of Gods and Heroes, and thousands of graves where the mountain foxes and hares peep at you. Red-hot in summer, freezing in winter, is that big, purple heather country of broken stone.

"Just when you think you are at the world's end, you see a smoke from East to West as far as the eye can turn, and then, under it, also as far as the eye can stretch, houses and temples, shops and theatres, barracks and granaries, trickling along like dice behind — always behind — one long, low, rising and falling, and hiding and showing line of towers. And that is the Wall!"

"Ah," said the children, taking breath.

"You may well," said Parnesius. "Old men who have followed the Eagles since boyhood say nothing in the Empire is more wonderful than first sight of the Wall!"

Eventually it falls to Parnesius and his friend Pertinax, whom he has first met in one of the "caves" of Mithras, to be responsible for the defence of the Wall, while their general, Maximus, who wants to be Emperor, denudes Britain, and even the ultimate rampart itself, of troops, so that he may fight Theodosius on the Continent. They understand the Picts beyond the Wall and manage them well enough. They even contrive first of all to drive off, and then to temporise with, the "Winged Hats" from the dark unknown North. At last the news comes that Maximus has failed and is dead. It is plain that they will have to withstand the attacks of Picts and "Winged Hats" without reinforcements and with a lively chance that, if they survive so long, Theodosius will kill them as he has killed their master. Then Parnesius says, "It conerns us to defend the Wall, no matter what Emperor dies or makes die".

Kipling has now elevated the Wall to the position of a major symbol. It is the bulwark of peace and good administration. Were it to be pierced there would ensue, first, all the brief horrors of conquest and rapine, and afterwards worse still, the generations — long horrors of incompetent barbarian rule. Therefore, although Parnesius and Pertinax know the defence to be well nigh hopeless, yet they must die rather than abandon it.

The point to be observed is that Kipling chooses a moment of time which makes his eulogy

The Prophet of Empire

of the Roman spirit at the same time an elegy upon it. It is here that we can see in its full development the change which began to come over his mind towards the end of the decade during which he was the recognised "Prophet of Empire". Some sort of foreboding, an ominous overtone, is already to be felt in the very sound as well as in the words of *Recessional*. Two years later the decisive experience of the South African War, as I shall try to show in a later chapter, completed the process of change.

Kipling, I repeat, never abandoned in the smallest degree the political philosophy which he had brought with him from India to a larger sphere. But as he grew older his advocacy of it grew less optimistic. A few years ago an attempt was made to prove that a revolution occurred in his own mind when his alleged incitements to military glory resulted in the death of his own son. That attempt was a little unfortunate, since it turned out, as soon as the facts were examined, that the story on which the theory was based had been written well before John Kipling was even posted as missing. Rudyard Kipling's hatred of the Germans had nothing to do with any personal loss. Its origins must be sought in years before ever a frontier had been crossed or a shot fired. Earlier than 1914 he had begun to pass into

Rudyard Kipling

the mood which made Pertinax say to Parnesius, "We be two dead men, my brother".

Unchangeable in his own soul, he was sensitive to the changes signalled by passing events. He believed, like the men on the Wall, that an assault on civilisation was impending. Not without reason did he, in the collected edition of his verse, set his poem on the outbreak of the Great War next after *Recessional*. It is the expression of the same mind meeting its own earlier forebodings in concrete form. It is not the poem of a man who rejoices in brute strength or slaughter for their own sake, not even that of the young man who did once think that war was a good if dangerous game:

> Once more we hear the word
> That sickened earth of old: —
> "No law except the Sword
> Unsheathed and uncontrolled."

It is the cry of a man summoning his fellows to a work of defence which is more vital than they may realise:

> For all we have and are,
> For all our children's fate,
> Stand up and take the war,
> The Hun is at the gate!

The Prophet of Empire

> Our world has passed away
> In wantonness o'erthrown.
> There is nothing left today
> But steel and fire and stone!
> Though all we knew depart,
> The old Commandments stand: —
> "In courage keep your heart,
> In strength lift up your hand."

And he says what there is to be defended:

> Comfort, content, delight,
> The ages' slow-bought gain.

The barbarians were mustering and — "It concerns us to defend the Wall".

But before 1914 he had already begun to think that the salvation of the world could not be left to the British Empire or even to a league of the English-speaking peoples. He had begun to dream of an effective combination of those elements in all nations which believe in orderly and peaceable government. If the Great War stirred him to a passion of hate, it was not because he himself had been bereaved by one of its incidental casualties. It was because he could see the Wall itself in danger. After the War was over he seemed sometimes to be rancorous and unforgiving, but that was because he believed that not all the breaches in the Wall had been repaired,

Rudyard Kipling

that the "breeds without" had not been brought within "the Law", and would sooner or later renew their assaults.

Our judgement of Kipling as a political thinker must depend, finally, on our interpretation of what he meant by "the Law". It is easy enough to produce a string of quotations to show that in his mind it meant no more than the supremacy of the people to which he happened to belong by birth. It would be as easy to match each of these quotations twice over by others proving that his master-thought, vaguely defined though it may have been at first, was very different.

The teaching of a man who almost invariably expresses his ideas in fiction or poetry is obviously difficult to reduce to a formula — and the attempt so to reduce it has its dangers. But the dangers and the difficulties must be braved, especially in a case where the issue has been so much confused by biassed and not always sincere criticism. "The Law" means that arrangement of life under which the common man is enabled to do the best which is in him for himself, his family and the rest of the world, including the generations yet to come. So far as civilisation has gone, that does not yet mean quite enough for everybody to eat. Under what we call civilisation, most people have more to eat than they formerly had

The Prophet of Empire

and fewer children are killed by famine and other avoidable disasters. We ought to advance from that point, but it is even more important to make sure that we do not recede from it. We have reached it with many pains and we hold to it precariously. The human race has before reached almost as high a level as we and has then fallen back. We are in danger of a similar recidivism.

When Kipling, in the early days of the Great War and before the word had become a popular term of abuse, cried, "The Hun is at the gate!" he meant it with all the force the cry might have had in the mouth of a Roman of the fifth century. He was not sticking out his tongue at the fellow-countrymen of Goethe and Heine, Kant and Planck, Mommsen and Wilamowitz-Moellendorff and saying to them, "Yah, you're a lot of Huns!" He was saying to his own fellow-countrymen, "Our enemies have slipped back to the standards of barbarism. The idea of civilisation, which you and I, consciously or unconsciously, have cherished, is in danger and it must be saved."

The historians of another generation will say how far he was right. It is for the commentators of his own time to point out what he really did say and to combat judgements founded on misunderstanding or prejudice.

I must return, I fear, for a moment to the

Rudyard Kipling

question of war. Kipling, like all the men born in his generation and for some years afterwards, was brought up in the tradition of colonial and frontier wars. In these the casualties were not heavy nor was the amount of incidental suffering high. To one thinking in such terms, it was still possible to consider warfare as an exercise tending to develop valuable personal qualities, and, at the same time, as something tending to spread the rule of law. Later, it was to him something to be dreaded and abhorred. Possibly what he had heard of conditions in the Russo-Japanese War influenced his opinion. His imagination would not have found it hard to make a reality out of the reports that came to him. But it remained something which was to be accepted with courage when the only alternative is the surrender of the right of the common man to do the best which is in him for himself, his family and the rest of the world, including the generations yet to come. Kipling changed his mind on many points of detail, his hopes for the future undoubtedly diminished, but his judgement of the proper aim of human effort was immutable.

It was necessary to make this long excursus on his political opinions for their own sake. I do not apologise for it. But it has also its bearing on his development as an artist. He was a little

The Prophet of Empire

arrogant as a young man, in his style and in the expression of his views — and who shall blame the possessor of such a talent? Then for the ten years of his great success he proceeded, without the arrogance which he no longer needed to spur him on, but still without learning humility. In the lives of great artists some such lesson is usually necessary. To many it comes, early or late, by way of some private crisis or disappointment. I suggest that to Kipling it came with the realisation that his hopes for the future of the world were not as well founded as he had supposed. He thought that the British people needed only exhortation to persuade it to serve "the Law" and make it prevail — and things turned out not to be as simple as that. This realisation began to present itself to him before the crucial days of the South African War. But that event, with its sequels, including the miserable Parliamentary history of the early years of the century and the General Election of 1906, which was a new dawn to some but certainly not to Kipling, made it unescapable. Before this happened, however, he enjoyed what may be called his first maturity.

CHAPTER IV

The First Maturity

From the point of view of the creative worker, Kipling lived in the 'Nineties through what most writers might have considered a fine Golden Age. The brilliant, the almost ominously brilliant, colours of his dawn cleared and steadied into a no less brilliant but more satisfying noontide light. What he had done already, remarkable as it was, must, by reason of his age, be regarded as a promise, even if a promise of a sort that is not often fulfilled. The critics waited, with a confidence which it would be impossible to regard as wholly unreasonable, for him not to fulfil it. But he did. He wrote both the *Jungle Book* and *Stalky & Co.*, the stories contained in the collections called *Life's Handicap, Many Inventions* and *The Day's Work*, and the poems contained in the collections called

The First Maturity

Barrack-room Ballads and *The Seven Seas*. He produced also three novels (one of them in collaboration) to which we shall come presently.

I do not think that even this formidable list contains the very finest of his work. But this period placed him in a category which, hard as it is to define, is easy to recognise. Mr. Maurice Baring has spoken of writers who are "safe in the Temple of Fame, which once you have entered you cannot leave. For this temple is like a wheel. It goes round and round, and sometimes some of its inmates are in the glare of the sun, and sometimes they are in the shade, but they are there; and they never fall out." Well before the turn of the century Kipling was safe in that Temple of Fame. As time goes by, his popularity and his reputation, as assessed by critical opinion, will, no doubt, fluctuate. So far as critical opinion goes, he has already spent some years on the shady side of the Temple. But it would be looking much too far ahead to imagine a day when he will not be considered one of the great writers of the English language.

It is a strange fact that failures bulk quite largely in the record of these triumphant years. It was not perhaps unnatural that he should endeavour once to write a full-length novel and no shame to him that he should fail in the attempt. But it

Rudyard Kipling

is something to be noticed that he should have tried twice again without improvement and then, succeeding at the fourth essay, outside our present decade, have abandoned the form for ever.

There is an obvious probability that the three failures, *The Light that Failed* (1891), *The Naulakha* (1892) and *Captains Courageous* (1897), were births of a desire to do what was expected of him, signs that the young prodigy did not even yet know quite how overwhelmingly powerful was the position which his gifts had secured for him. There is an additional and rather startling sign of this in the history of the first of these novels. It made its appearance in book form with a tell-tale note: "This is the story of *The Light that Failed* as it was originally conceived by the writer — Rudyard Kipling". In other words, the fact that the blind Dick Heldar should not get his Maisie and should go instead to look for death in the Sudan was too much for the editor of *Lippincott's Magazine,* and the author bowed to the need for a happier ending. Kipling makes some remarks about this book in his reminiscences but he does not mention this incident. It would have been interesting to have had his comment on it.

Now there is no imperative artistic fitness about the conclusion of *The Light that Failed*. The conclusion which Kipling gave to it can be

The First Maturity

condemned as at once arbitrary and obvious. Perhaps the story itself has not sufficient weight or design to lead to any conclusion of real significance, but a better might easily have been devised. So far the editor of *Lippincott's Magazine* may be said to have had reason on his side. But Kipling's yielding was not due to the fact that as an artist he had been convinced. He restored his own tragic end as soon as he had no magazine-editor to please. He committed, to use plain words, the same sin as Dick Heldar in the book. Dick did a picture for a weekly paper of a rifleman as "a flushed, dishevelled, bedevilled scallawag with his helmet at the back of his head, and the living fear of death in his eye, and the blood oozing out of a cut over his ankle-bone. He wasn't pretty, but he was all soldier and very much man." But:

The art-manager of that abandoned paper said that his subscribers wouldn't like it. It was brutal and coarse and violent, — man being naturally gentle when he's fighting for his life. They wanted something more restful with a little more colour. I could have said a good deal, but you might as well talk to a sheep as an art-manager. I took my "Last Shot" back. Behold the result! I put him into a lovely red coat without a speck on it. That is Art. I polished his boots, — observe the high light on the toe. That is Art. I cleaned his rifle, — rifles are always clean on active service, — because that is indispensable to Art. I pipe-clayed his helmet, — pipeclay is always used on active service, and is indispensable to Art. I shaved his chin, I washed his hands, and gave him an air of fatted peace. Result, military tailor's fashion-plate. Price, thank Heaven, twice as much as for the first sketch, which was moderately decent.

Torpenhow put his foot through the revised canvas. But Kipling's revised novel was published.

But, apart altogether from this matter of the ending of it, *The Light that Failed* shows Kipling as a novelist who is not on the same plane as the writer of short stories. It has fine things in it, and good things, and readable things, but no coherent unity. It sets out, in the first place, to tell the story of two human beings over a considerable period of time. Dick and Maisie are together as children, and a link is then made between them which is to affect them both when they meet later in grown-up days. The childhood passages owe a great deal to that episode in Kipling's own childhood, which, as we now know, he has described in more detail in *Baa, Baa, Black Sheep*. Mrs. Jennett's way of bringing up the small boy who had been given to her care was such that "where he looked for love she gave him first aversion and then hate. Where he, growing older, had sought a little sympathy, she gave him ridicule."

The First Maturity

When he grew older he was sent to school, but "in the holidays he returned to the teachings of Mrs. Jennett, and, that the chain of discipline might not be weakened by association with the world, was generally beaten, on one count or another, before he had been twelve hours under her roof". But he had "a companion in bondage", Maisie, whose "chiefest friend on earth" was the goat, Amomma. Mrs. Jennett threatened the goat.

"Then," said the atom, choosing her words very deliberately, "I shall write to my lawyer-peoples and tell them that you are a very bad woman. Amomma is mine, mine, mine!" Mrs. Jennett made a movement to the hall, where certain umbrellas and canes stood in a rack. The atom understood as clearly as Dick what this meant. "I have been beaten before," she said, still in the same passionless voice; "I have been beaten worse than you can ever beat me. If you beat me I shall write to my lawyer-peoples and tell them that you do not give me enough to eat. I am not afraid of you." Mrs. Jennett did not go into the hall, and the atom, after a pause to assure herself that all danger of war was past, went out, to weep bitterly on Amomma's neck.

Now the Dick of these preliminary pages might have easily developed into the Dick of the rest of the story — though the development would have been more convincing if we had been told more about the intervening stages. But the Maisie of the later chapters might just as well be somebody else. The only real connection between the two Maisies is that Dick felt very strongly about them both. It is impossible to believe that the decisive and strong-charactered child who so well defended herself and Amomma could have grown into the feebly obstinate girl who fails Dick for want of decision and clings to a vocation in which she has no real hope of success but from which she still hopes to obtain a few laudatory press-cuttings. Kipling insists, he makes both Dick and her insist, on the second Maisie's strength of will. But the insistence is never convincing. Maisie is simply an *ad hoc* character. She is a person rather perfunctorily invented to make the hero unhappy.

It is ill work guessing, with no better foundation than internal evidence and a general knowledge of the circumstances, how an author came to write a book which is perceptibly below what might have been expected of him. But some explanation of *The Light That Failed* must be offered, and mine may put in a better light at least one passage which has drawn unfavourable comment. I do not believe that Kipling ever really wanted to write this story or that he enjoyed writing it or that he was satisfied with it when it

The First Maturity

was done. His own remarks on it at the end of his life are rather of an exculpatory nature. I guess, though of course it must be understood that this is no more than a guess, that he felt that at this stage in his career he ought to write a novel, that the feeling was converted into a serious temptation by an offer from a magazine and that he was committed to the enterprise before he had given it much thought.

For the most part the book is a series of brilliant vampings on themes collected from here and there, a patchwork quilt made out of oddments in the author's work-basket. The first chapter is essentially, as I have already said, another version, not so well done, of *Baa, Baa, Black Sheep*. Dick Heldar's success is very obviously based on Kipling's own and we may surmise that the warnings addressed to Dick by his friends resemble those cannily addressed by Kipling to himself. The end is simply the effort of a brilliant writer with unlimited energy and unlimited technical capacity to get to an end somehow. This, I believe, is the true explanation of Dick's hysterical exclamations when the raiders are repulsed by a machine-gun in the armoured train from Suakim — "God is very good — I never thought I'd hear this again. Give 'em hell, men. Oh, give 'em hell!" and "It was a lark, though. I only wish it had

Rudyard Kipling

lasted twice as long. How superb it must have looked from outside."

"This," said Le Gallienne, "is the bellowing of mere homicidal lust," and it, as much as anything else, led him to remark that "for the most part Mr. Kipling's work is an appeal to, and a vindication of, the Englishman as brute." There is one obvious defence to be made. It can be said that at this moment Dick was ill-balanced and hysterical, for perfectly comprehensible reasons. His creator did no more than set down his behaviour truthfully. But to me it seems that the shrillness of these unpleasant yelps is Kipling's own. He did the best he could to carry off the unsatisfactory finish of an unsatisfactory book by a display of violence. He is effectively rebuked on the same page when the Lieutenant of Sappers gives his reason for using the machine-gun — "They'll be playing old Harry with my permanent way if we don't stop 'em." That is the real Kipling.

Yet, if one were not comparing this book with the Kipling of, say, *The Man Who Would Be King*, how natural it would be to shift the emphasis, and say no more than that parts of it are superb! Whatever parts of his task he may have failed in, Kipling did not fail in his description of Dick's disaster. Not even he often surpassed that height

The First Maturity

of virtuosity in which he put into the mouth of the newly blind man who is objecting to being taken out, the simple words, "Besides . . . something will run over me."

It is not possible to say quite so much of the next of his novels. *The Naulahka*, which he wrote in collaboration with his brother-in-law, Wolcott Balestier, is a goodish story, a readable story, with some attractive scenes and characters, but it is nothing more. Again it conveys the impression that the author set to work without giving his plan sufficient consideration in advance. It is the story of Nick Tarvin who has two ambitions in life. One is to boost his home-town, Topaz, Colorado. The other is to marry Kate Sheriff. These two combine to send him to Rhatore, the capital of a native state in Rajputana. The combination is unhappily so far-fetched as to throw a shadow over the enjoyment of the whole book. It is natural enough that Kate should be seized by a vocation to tend the unhappy women of India and that in pursuit of it she should go to the mission at Rhatore. But is it equally natural that Tarvin, wishing the Three Company's Railway to construct a junction at Topaz, should undertake to secure for the wife of the President of the Railway the legendary state jewel of Rhatore — the Naulahka? Such jewels are not for sale and Tarvin is

Rudyard Kipling

not represented as being a thief. In the end he does acquire the Naulahka by dishonest means but, Kate having now surrendered to his wooing, he realises that to keep it would make him unworthy of her. He returns it and goes back to Topaz, married but otherwise empty-handed. We are not told how he explains to the President's wife his failure to keep his promise to her or how he justifies to his fellow-citizens his confident boast that he will secure the junction for them. We are not even told whether Topaz got the junction or not. The return of Nick and Kate to their native place is not described. We are merely left unable to believe that he did not know from the first that the enterprise was impossible.

What is best in the book is the description of life in a native state, a subject which Kipling did not touch elsewhere. The commercial travellers, representing the King's creditors, wait day after day at the rest-house, hoping for a little on account. The King, refreshing himself with opium and a mixture of brandy and champagne, laments that the English Resident would make a fuss if he killed anyone. In the women's quarters of the palace the new Queen, a gipsy woman, plots against the life of the heir apparent, the little Maharaj Kunwar, whose mother, the old Queen, knows how little she can do for his protection.

The First Maturity

This last situation produces the most poignant pages in the story. The Maharaj brings a present to Kate from his mother, "a crude yellow and black comforter, with a violent crimson fringe, clumsily knitted," and a message which he repeats twice:

"My mother, the Queen — the real Queen — says: 'I was three months at this work. It is for you, because I have seen your face. That which has been made may be unravelled against our will, and a gipsy's hands are always picking. For the love of the gods look to it that a gipsy unravels nothing that I have made, for it is my life and soul to me. Protect this work of mine that comes from me — a cloth nine years upon the loom.' I know more English than my mother," said the child, dropping into his ordinary speech.

It is Tarvin who reads the riddle and says, "Can't you see what it means? It's the boy — the cloth nine years on the loom", whereupon Kate exclaims, weeping, "O Nick! what shall we do in this horrible country?" Then:

"Ah!" said the Maharaj, utterly unmoved, "I was to go when I saw that you cried." He lifted up his voice for the carriage and troopers, and departed leaving the shabby comforter on the floor.

Rudyard Kipling

The passage which nearest approaches this in power is the story of Tarvin's visit in search of the Naulahka, to the dead city of Gunnaur, where:

The last house ended in a heap of ruins among a tangle of mimosa and tall grass, through which ran a narrow foot-track. Tarvin marked the house as the first actual ruin he had seen. His complaint against all the others, the temples and the palaces, was that they were not ruined, but dead — empty, swept, and garnished, with the seven devils of loneliness in riotous possession. In time — in a few thousand years perhaps — the city would crumble away. He was distinctly glad that one house at least had set the example.

There are two incidental points about the book which deserve to be noticed before we pass on. One of them is that much of it is given to a description of those miseries of women's life under the Hindu code which Miss Margaret Mayo raised a storm by describing more than a quarter of a century later. The other is that we find here examples of two slang-words which are generally supposed to be of much later date. Tarvin says to the commercial travellers at the rest-house, "What's your lay? What's your racket?" And the Maharaj says, "The hospital has all gone *phut*."

It will be noticed that I have written of *The Naulahka* as though Kipling were the sole author of it. His brother-in-law and collaborator, Wol-

The First Maturity

cott Balestier, was a writer who died young, said by those who knew him best to have been of brilliant unfulfilled promise. Internal evidence offers no suggestion as to his share, whether for good or evil, in the partnership. There is little, if anything, here which Kipling might not have written, and the weaknesses of the book are not those of collaboration but such as Kipling was quite capable of committing unaided.

The scene of the first of these novels was mostly in London, partly in the Sudan. That of the second was partly in America, mostly in India. That of the third was almost wholly on the Grand Banks of Newfoundland. *Captains Courageous* is often mentioned as though it had been written as a story of adventure for boys. It is true enough that boys do like it, and Kipling may have planned it with some such idea in his head. But if he had formed the idea very clearly, he would, I think, have written the opening conversation in the liner's smoking-room in a slightly different, rather less adult key. The subject of the conversation is Harvey Cheyne, son of a busy millionaire and an adoring mother, of whom one passenger says that he is "the biggest nuisance aboard", and another that: "He's more to be pitied than anything . . . they've dragged him around from hotel to hotel ever since he was a kid. I was talking to his mother this morning. She's a lovely lady, but she don't pretend to manage him." Harvey then makes his appearance, which is painted in with rather a loaded brush. He is under sixteen and his pocket-money is two hundred dollars a month. He suggests to the occupants of the smoking-room that they should make up a game of poker with him and remarks, "You can hear the fish-boats squawking all round us. Say, wouldn't it be great if we ran down one?"

This highly disagreeable little creature is presently washed overboard and rescued by one of the "fish-boats". The skipper, Disko Troop, of the *We're Here* of Gloucester, dislikes his manners and refuses to believe his stories of his father's wealth. He refuses also to take the *We're Here* immediately to New York and tells Harvey that he will engage him as a hand for the rest of the fishing-season at ten and a half dollars a month. When Harvey shrilly and insultingly refuses the offer, Disko dispassionately knocks him into the scuppers. This is the end of Chapter One.

Now the story of the redemption of Harvey Cheyne could have been convincingly told, though it would have been in the earlier stages an almost unbearably cruel business. Or a story-teller anxious not to harrow the feelings of his readers excessively might have passed over the early stages in a sum-

The First Maturity

mary with a few vivid pictures — which no one could have done better than Kipling. He shows us instead the process completed in five pages and about half an hour's conversation between Harvey and Disko's son, Dan. After that, Harvey is a reformed character, humble and anxious to learn, with all the nonsense knocked out of him. No novel can survive unhurt so light-hearted a slap in the face of obvious truth. There is another impossibility in the short space of time in which Harvey, soft, cigarette-smoking, pasty-faced, utterly out of condition, adapts himself to the physical rigours of life in the fishing-fleet. He would, in fact, have suffered very serious bodily agony.

If he is to enjoy *Captains Courageous* as it can be enjoyed the reader must assume that the author has done something for him which, in fact, has not been done. He must assume that the transformation of the millionaire's spoilt child has been accomplished in due agreement with what is likely. Then he will be free to appreciate a racy account of an unfamiliar kind of life and of some agreeable characters. Here we have Kipling at one of his bests. These are men doing their own specialised job and he rejoices in the competence with which they do it. It is so vivid that one can hardly believe he was not there himself. But the detail came from a doctor who had once worked

Rudyard Kipling

in the fishing-fleet. Under the doctor's guidance Kipling made enquiries on the water-front and in sailors' eating-houses. And his mentor "sent me — may he be forgiven! — out on a pollock-fisher, which is ten times fouler than any cod-schooner, and I was immortally sick, even though they tried to revive me with a fragment of unfresh pollock." It is his delight in professional expertness which enables him to bridge the gulf between report and first-hand knowledge. This appears again and again throughout *Captains Courageous*, as when he describes how Disko Troop knew where it was best to fish and how he was able once again to take the *We're Here* back to Gloucester a week in front of the rest of the fleet. And there is another of his bests in many enchanting pictures of a small ship among big seas. Here is one of them:

> The little schooner was gambolling all around her anchor among the silver-tipped waves. Backing with a start of affected surprise at the sight of the strained cable, she pounced on it like a kitten, while the spray of her descent burst through the hawse-holes with the report of a gun. Shaking her head, she would say: "Well, I'm sorry I can't stay any longer with you. I'm going North," and would sidle off, halting suddenly with a dramatic rattle of her rigging. "As I was just going to observe," she would begin, as gravely as a

The First Maturity

drunken man addressing a lamp-post. The rest of the sentence (she acted her words in dumb-show, of course) was lost in a fit of fidgets, when she behaved like a puppy chewing a string, a clumsy woman in a side-saddle, a hen with her head cut off, or a cow stung by a hornet, exactly as the whims of the sea took her.

"See her sayin' her piece. She's Patrick Henry naow," said Dan.

She swung sideways on a roller, and gesticulated with her jib-boom from port to starboard.

"But — ez — fer — me, give me liberty — er give me — death!"

Wop! She sat down in the moon-path on the water, curtseying with a flourish of pride impressive enough had not the wheel-gear sniggered mockingly in its box.

The contemporary critics of these three novels made a stricture on them with which it would be hard to argue. They were, these critics said, the work of a writer of short stories whose gift for characterisation was not equal to the severe test which a full-length novel imposes. In each of the three the author asked the reader to accept a fundamental fact without giving him any plausible reason why he should accept it. He asked the reader to believe that the first Maisie who stood so gallantly by Amomma grew into the second

Maisie who ran away from Dick in his agony. He asked him to believe that Nick Tarvin was prepared to commit a common theft. He asked him to believe that Harvey Cheyne was changed to the roots of his soul by a blow on the nose. And, in each case, it is too much for any reader to be asked to believe. There was material for a short story in each book — the artist's blindness, the cloth nine years on the loom, the work and the gaiety of the fishing-fleet. But Kipling, stepping on to territory where he was not at home, began each book in fatal hesitation.

The three novels did not hurt his reputation. They might indeed have made that of another man. But, if they had been representative of the work he did in the 'Nineties, it would have been necessary to conclude that he was making no important advance as an artist and natural to suppose that some retrogression might be expected. They did, indeed, show signs of wider range and greater flexibility of style, as well as of an ability to write about things that happened outside India. But the novel which was expected of him during these ten years was still to come, though it came not long after they had expired. Meanwhile he moved on to a new level of achievement in those fields in which he had already established himself — the short story and poetry.

The First Maturity

II

It was, in fact, the short stories and the poems which Kipling wrote during this year which established him in the place from which he cannot be dislodged. There were more Indian stories. With these, one series of them excepted, we need not concern ourselves. But there was a wide extension of the geographical field of his interests. Some of that has been seen already in *Captains Courageous*. He had learnt to see the American continent as something more than a tract of land which the traveller wonderingly crosses. He had also discovered London.

Of this he has left an unexpected proof in *The Record of Badalia Herodsfoot*. This not very good story is an almost unparalleled example of Kipling being led by fashion in the choice of his material. That was a time when a good many authors were turning to "mean streets" in search of romance and tragedy and, for once, Kipling turned with the rest. (Perhaps it was due to something that Henley said to him.) Badalia was an inhabitant of the East End:

In the beginning of things she had been unregenerate; had worn the heavy fluffy fringe which is the ornament of the costermonger's girl, and there is a

Rudyard Kipling

legend in Gunnison Street that on her wedding-day she, a flare-lamp in either hand, danced dances on a discarded lover's winkle-barrow, till a policeman interfered, and then Badalia danced with the Law amid shoutings. These were her days of fatness, and they did not last long, for her husband after two years took to himself another woman, and passed out of Badalia's life, over Badalia's senseless body, for he stifled protest with blows.

She is killed by her husband, defending from him the money with which she has been entrusted as a sort of unofficial missioner. This was Kipling's first and last attempt to make himself at home with the city-dwellers of his own country. Possibly he made this uncharacteristic excursion only to show that he could do it as well as the others. He never seems quite at home in it, though he speaks with characteristic air of omniscience of "a second marriage according to the customs of Gunnison Street, which do not differ from those of the Barralong". My own guess is that his one dip into the slums rather flummoxed him. He could think of nothing to be done with slum-dwellers so long as they continued to dwell in the slums. And the only way out he could see at that time was, for men alone, the way into the Army. This was a sterile answer, so he turned his eyes elsewhere. It gives a key to what is

The First Maturity

wanting in his first maturity that he came so close to this essential problem and then left it.

Having left it, he turned his eyes on the world at large, finding everywhere nourishment for a greater hope. The Indian stories, the late harvest of an early experience, stress firmly the necessity of a ruling class — a class the members of which deserve to rule because they consider the honourable performance of the job a thing better than life itself. Findlayson, in *The Bridge-Builders*, is an example of those men whom Kipling at this time expected to take the world somewhere.

The Bridge-Builders is a story crammed with technicalities. Findlayson's work was:

One mile and three-quarters in length; a lattice-girder bridge, trussed with the Findlayson truss, standing on seven-and-twenty brick piers. Each one of those piers was twenty-four feet in diameter, capped with red Agra stone and sunk eighty feet below the shifting sand of the Ganges' bed.

It survived the flood in the river.

But this story is by no means alone in its wealth of technicalities. Kipling, during this period of his life, did seem to revel in machinery for its own sake. There is one passage which has been severely criticised on this ground. It occurs in a story called *The Devil and the Deep Sea*, in which an English pearl-poaching ship is pursued

Rudyard Kipling

by a foreign cruiser which fires a shell at her. The whole description is much too long to quote here. I take out of it only a piece:

> The forward engine had no more work to do. The released piston-rod, therefore, drove up fiercely, with nothing to check it, and started most of the nuts of the cylinder-cover. It came down again, the full weight of the steam behind it, and the foot of the disconnected connecting-rod, useless as the leg of a man with a sprained ankle, flung out to the right and struck the starboard, or right-hand, cast-iron supporting column of the forward engine, cracking it clean through about six inches above the base, and wedging the upper portion outwards three inches towards the ship's side. There the connecting-rod jammed. Meantime, the after-engine, being as yet unembarrassed, went on with its work, and in so doing brought round at its next revolution the crank of the forward engine, which smote the already jammed connecting-rod, bending it and therewith the piston-rod cross-head — the big cross-piece that slides up and down so smoothly.

This is, on the face of it, rather a mouthful to swallow. At the same time it moves fast, and it gives an impression of disaster which could not have been conveyed by the bald statement that the engines had been put out of action. It produces the necessary effect, and that might seem to be all that is necessary to say about it.

The First Maturity

But there are two or three other things to be said about Kipling's use of technical details. Undoubtedly he loved them, and he dealt in them to an extent which sometimes drew ridicule upon him. The extreme of it is to be found in *With the Night Mail* where he revelled in the technicalities of machinery that had not yet been, and was not ever likely to be, invented. We are in the engine-room of an Air Postal Packet in the year 2000 A.D.:

Here we find Fleury's Paradox of the Bulk-headed Vacuum — which we accept now without thought — literally in full blast. The three engines are H.T. and T. assisted-vacuo Fleury turbines running from 3000 to the Limit — that is to say, up to the point when the blades make the air "bell" — cut out a vacuum for themselves precisely as over-driven marine propellers used to do. "162's" Limit is low on account of the small size of her nine screws, which, though handier than the old colloid Thelussons, "bell" sooner. The midships engine, generally used as a reinforce, is not running; so the port and starboard turbine vacuum-chambers draw direct into the return-mains.

"Revelling" is, I think, the right word. Thus do young authors assuage their urgent desires by writing descriptions of imaginary women who are both beautiful and kind. There was never enough machinery in the world, of the sort that makes for security and prosperity, to satisfy Kipling's avid imagination.

But there was quite enough to provide him with a vehicle for the gospel which now most of all he was anxious to preach — the gospel of co-ordinated work, the gospel of discipline for useful ends, the gospel of the holiness of function. It served for verse as well as for prose. *M'Andrew's Hymn* made a sensation when it was first printed. It was slightly shocking that the sacred medium of verse should be used for references to follower-bolts and snifter-rods. At the same time it was quite impossible to overlook the power and the cogency of the poem. Kipling probably did not think that he had done anything unusual. Browning had been dead a bare four years, and it was from Browning that he derived this device of presenting a philosophy in a richly decorated soliloquy. I do not remember when any critic last expressed an opinion on this piece. But it is hardly to be believed that its vigorous virtues can be denied, or that anyone can overlook the fact that it does present a view of life with all of the efficiency that it praises:

I'm sick of all their quirks an' turns — the loves an'
    doves they dream —
Lord, send a man like Robbie Burns to sing the Song
    o' Steam!

The First Maturity

To match wi' Scotia's noblest speech yon orchestra sublime
Whaurto — uplifted like the Just — the tail-rods mark the time.
The crank-throws give the double-bass, the feed-pump sobs an' heaves,
An' now the main eccentrics start their quarrel on the sheaves:
Her time, her own appointed time, the rocking link-head bides,
Till — hear that note? — the rod's return whings glimmerin' through the guides.
They're all awa'! True beat, full power, the clangin' chorus goes
Clear to the tunnel where they sit, my purrin' dynamoes.
Interdependence absolute, foreseen, ordained, decreed,
To work, Ye'll note, at ony tilt an' every rare o' speed.
Fra' skylight-lift to furnace-bars, backed, bolted, braced an' stayed,
An' singin' like the Mornin' Stars for joy that they are made;
While, out o' touch o' vanity, the sweatin' thrust-block says:
"Not unto us the praise, or man — not unto us the praise!"
Now, a' together, hear them lift their lesson — theirs an' mine:
"Law, Orrder, Duty an' Restraint, Obedience, Discipline!"

Rudyard Kipling

The moral which is here stated is expounded further in two of the stories written during this time. One of them describes the maiden-voyage of the *Dimbula*, a cargo-steamer of twelve hundred tons, of which her skipper says cautiously, "I'm sayin' that it takes more than christenin' to mak' a ship. In the nature of things, Miss Frazier, if you follow me, she's just irons and rivets and plates put into the form of a ship. She has to find herself yet."[1] Thus, throughout the voyage from Liverpool to New York, the different parts of the ship talk volubly about their new and unhappy experiences:

"It isn't distressingly calm now," said the extra-strong frames — they were called web-frames — in the engine-room. "There's an upward thrust that we don't understand, and there's a twist that is very bad for our brackets and diamond-plates, and there's a sort of west-north-westerly pull that follows the twist, which seriously annoys us. We mention this because we happened to cost a good deal of money, and we feel sure that the owner would not approve of our being treated in this frivolous way."

"I'm afraid the matter is out of the owner's hands for the present," said the Steam, slipping into the con-

---

[1] This was a novel conception to most of those who read the story when it was first published. It is a commonplace to the generation of today which is used to the running-in of new cars. The spread of knowledge would have pleased Kipling.

The First Maturity

denser. "You're left to your own devices till the weather betters."

But as the voyage goes on, discoveries begin to be made:

"We have made a most amazing discovery," said the stringers, one after another. "A discovery that entirely changes the situation. We have found, for the first time in the history of ship-building, that the inward pull of the deck-beams and the outward thrust of the frames lock us, as it were, more closely in our places, and enable us to endure a strain which is entirely without parallel in the records of marine architecture."

Then comes the entry into New York harbour:

A new, big voice said slowly and thickly, as though the owner had just waked up: "It's my conviction that I have made a fool of myself."

The Steam knew what had happened at once; for when a ship finds herself all the talking of the separate pieces ceases and melts into one voice, which is the soul of the ship.

"Who are you?" he said, with a laugh.

"I am the *Dimbula*, of course. I've never been anything else except that — and a fool!"

Then again in *.007*, we have an exact companion piece to this, written in the same style

Rudyard Kipling

and with the same purpose. It describes the first day in the working life of a young locomotive on an American line:

> With a very quavering voice he whistled for his first grade crossing (an event in the life of a locomotive) and his nerves were in no way restored by the sight of a frantic horse and a white-faced man in a buggy less than a yard from his right shoulder. Then he was sure he would jump the track; felt his flanges mounting the rail at every curve; knew that his first grade would make him lie down even as Comanche had done at the Newton's.

These were, of course, exciting stories in an almost wholly novel vein and written with a quite novel smoothness of execution. They were popular. And, as a matter of fact, the ordinary reader so far from being repelled by technicalities actually has a liking for them if they are described to him with a convincing ease and fluency. We all like being told how things work. These stories leave us feeling that now we know more about steamships and locomotives than we ever did before. It is true that gaps and slips in Kipling's knowledge have been detected, even in his knowledge of the army. He once, I think, described a corporal as wearing a sash, which caused a great deal of military indignation. He has himself confessed

The First Maturity

to one gigantic bloomer, somewhere in his works, which no one has yet discovered. This should be a sort of Everest peak for the ambitious investigator. It remains, however, the wonder that he was able to assimilate and transmit so much complicated knowledge rather than that here and there he should have been in error.

But they are more than exciting stories, fairy-stories of a new kind. They are further examples of Kipling's untiring insistence on the importance of the job. The *Dimbula* is a symbol of members of an organisation learning to work together, the locomotive .007 of an individual learning to take responsibility. Possibly it was in the collection in which they are included, that, as its title, *The Day's Work*, suggests, he reached his greatest insistence on this master-idea. Another story here is *The Bridge-Builders*, which I have already quoted. Yet another is *Bread Upon the Waters*, in which Chief Engineer McPhee is dismissed by his Board for refusing to run the *Breslau* on her new time schedule. He opens his heart to McRimmon, another ship-owner, who affects to chide him:

"Hoot, oot," said he. "Ye might ha' crammed her a little — enough to show ye were drivin' her — an' brought her in twa days behind. What's easier than to say ye slowed for bearin's, eh? All my men do it, and — I believe 'em."

"McRimmon," says I, "what's her virginity to a lassie?"

He puckered his dry face an' twisted in his chair. "The warld an' a'," says he. "My God, the vara warld an' a'! But what ha' you or me to do wi' virginity, this late along?"

"This," I said. "There's just one thing that each one of us in his trade or profession will *not* do for ony consideration whatever. If I run to time I run to time, barrin' always the risks o' the high seas. Less than that, under God, I have not done. More than that, by God, I will not do!"

And there is yet another story in which Kipling approaches the matter from another and what is for him an unusual, point of view. *The Maltese Cat* is a tale of polo, told almost exclusively as the ponies see it. These are animals who have been trained to one purpose and concentrate on it. They ought to win, the Cat assures his colleagues, in spite of the odds against them, because they know the game and play it with their heads and know how to play together.

The special question which this tale makes us ask arises out of its uniqueness. Nowhere else in all the range of his work has Kipling given serious attention to the playing of games. His other

The First Maturity

allusions to sports of any kind might almost be collected into half-a-dozen pages. So far as I can recollect his only noteworthy reference to golf is the remark which would probably appear strange to Mr. Bobby Jones and Mr. Walter Hagen, as well as to a number of Englishmen whom they have out-driven, that "When an American knows the innermost meaning of 'Don't press, slow back, and keep your eye on the ball,' he is, for practical purposes, denationalised". The verses he wrote in 1898 for a series of pictures of various sports must have been written to oblige a friend and are perfunctory and almost entirely without merit. Cricket and football do not appear (with one exception) apart from the house-matches which Stalky, Turkey and Beetle so deeply despised. Hunting appears now and again, racing not at all after the Indian stories, and tennis never.

Now we know that Kipling, owing to his defective sight, was never able to play any games at all. His only form of athletic exercise was swimming. (About this, too, oddly enough, in spite of Swinburne's example, he wrote next to nothing.) But this hardly explains his almost complete neglect of the favourite recreations of just the sort of Englishman whom he most admires and most needs for the recruitment of his desired governing class. It seems impossible not to suspect that his schooldays gave a distinct moulding to his mind in this respect. There is no discoverable reason why he should not have written about other games in the same way as about polo. They would have provided him with the technicalities he loved and with opportunities for driving home the lesson which he desired to teach. But we encounter here an almost completely blind spot.

Take, for example, football as it appears in *Stalky & Co.*, remembering that, in his time, the United Services College was one of the finest Rugger schools in the west of England. In one of these stories, *A Little Prep.*, the Head "ruins" the First Fifteen by claiming four of its members for extra-tuition. The remedy adopted for this disaster is rather extraordinary. "Let's promote all the Second Fifteen," says the Head of Games, "and make Big Side play up." How the whole of the Second Fifteen could be promoted into four vacancies is more than I can pretend to understand, and I incline to believe that Kipling not only had no idea of what he meant but also did not much care whether what he said meant anything — a carelessness which was exceedingly unlike him. In the upshot, Turkey is given a place in the First Fifteen for the Old Boys' match and Stalky plays as substitute for the Old Boys. This reminds the reader rather abruptly that, so far as we can rely

The First Maturity

on the book for evidence, neither of them has ever played, even for his House, let alone for the Second Fifteen. There is, in fact, no suggestion elsewhere that they ever played football at all, though equally there is no suggestion that they were for any reason exempted from it, as Beetle was. This does amount to a falsification of the background, more especially since Beetle's constant companions must have been regularly taken away from him by compulsory games — a falsification all the more remarkable in that it has every air of having been committed quite unconsciously.

III

This is, to be sure, not a point to be much laboured, since, as we have already seen, *Stalky & Co.* is in effect a collection of fairy-stories. In one sense, these three were more like real boys than the boys found up to then in most school-stories. In another sense, they were unlike any boys that ever existed. Certainly we know beyond all dispute that they were not like the three boys at the United Services College who were called Dunsterville, Beresford and Kipling. They are what Kipling would have liked himself and his companions to be. They are larger than life. They

Rudyard Kipling

are myths. And there was a good deal of the myth-maker about Kipling at this time. To the exploits of his predecessors in this *genre*, who had created talking animals, he had added machines that talked. His schoolboys were not perhaps, on the face of it, quite so extraordinary as this, but they were in the same line of imaginative creation. And so we find it also in other stories which are roughly contemporary with these. Their characters are larger than life. Their events are as gigantic as Brocken-spectres.

The most famous of these is, I suppose, the incomparable *"Brugglesmith"*. But different men have their own favourites. My own happens to be *My Sunday at Home*. But unquestionably the most gigantic of them in plan and in execution is *The Village that Voted the Earth Was Flat*. This was, in fact, written, or at any rate finished, in 1913. But in both mood and style it is really the climax of what Kipling created in the 'Nineties. Like so much of what he did it shows traces of his having learnt from others: there are traces of Bret Harte and the Stevenson of *The Wrong Box*, and some perhaps of Mark Twain. But, as always, when he learnt from others, the result is his own. This particular form of the huge and elaborate practical joke in words belongs to Kipling. He

The First Maturity

enjoyed making it with a gusto that never got out of control, that indeed did, in its intensity combined with the strictness of the artistic control imposed on it, carry it rather beyond the limits of a joke.

Kipling lavishes so much in the way of invention and style on *The Village that Voted the Earth Was Flat* as to make it in the end almost terrifying. Nowhere better than in the fifty-odd pages of this story can one see his power over language used to a deliberately cumulative purpose. Certain motorists are grossly offended by the behaviour on the local Bench of Sir Thomas Ingell, the Squire of Huckley. They determine in revenge to make him and Huckley ridiculous. One is a newspaper-proprietor, another a music-hall impresario, a third a member of Parliament. The purpose of their collaboration is expressed by Bat Masquerier, when he says: "Gentlemen, when our combination has finished with Sir Thomas Ingell, Bart., M.P. and everything else that is his, Sodom and Gomorrah will be a winsome bit of Merrie England beside 'em". How this is achieved need not be told here. But we must pause for a moment to see how Kipling uses all his resources of language to appal the reader with the colossal extent of the joke, especially in his use of similes. Here are a

Rudyard Kipling

few examples, taken from three consecutive pages of this story:

The song, pinned down by the faithful double-basses as the bull-dog pins down the bellowing bull. . . .

Still the song, through all those white-washed walls, shook the reinforced concrete of the Trefoil as steam pile-drivers shake the flanks of a dock. . . .

Now it was more like mine-pumps in flood.

A few days passed which were like nothing except, perhaps, a suspense of fever in which the sick man perceives the searchlights of the world's assembled navies in act to converge on one minute fragment of wreckage—one only in all the black and agony-strewn sea.

Then, in all the zealous, merciless Press, Huckley was laid out for [the world] to look at, as a drop of pond-water is exposed on the sheet of a magic-lantern show.

Olyett and I did not need to lift our little fingers any more than the Alpine climber whose last sentence has unkeyed the arch of the avalanche. The thing roared and pulverised and swept beyond eyesight all by itself.

But popular favour, in choosing *"Brugglesmith"* out of these stories for the greatest fame, has probably done well. It is, though elaborately wrought, less elaborate than *The Village that Voted the Earth Was Flat* and in that degree more

The First Maturity

spontaneous in its effect. Here we are translated into the serene upper skies of pure farce where anything may happen and the most surprising things done. McPhee's[1] drunken guest on board the *Breslau* heaps every conceivable discomfort and indignity on the narrator who, alone with him in a dinghy in the Pool, has nevertheless time and impartiality enough to enjoy "an exhibition of first-class steering". What follows is drunkenness raised to the celestial plane. "Brugglesmith" rises in the bows of the dinghy and declaims:

> Ye Towers o' Julia, London's lasting wrong,
> > By mony a foul an' midnight murder fed —
> Sweet Thames, run softly till I end my song —
> > And yon's the grave as little as my bed.

adding, "I'm a poet mysel' an' I can feel for others". (This passage, by the way, once appeared in the scholarship examination papers of an eminent College under the familiar injunction: "Assign the following to its author on grounds of style".) The couple are picked up by a police-boat and taken to a flat, where "Brugglesmith" demands drink which is refused him:

I heard my companion say angrily to a constable, "If you will not give it to a dry man, ye maun to a

---

[1] This must be our old friend McPhee, who salvaged the *Grothou*, although here he appears as "M'Phee." I have taken the liberty of altering the spelling.

drookit." Then he walked deliberately off the edge of the flat into the water. Somebody stuck a boat-hook into his clothes and hauled him out.

"Now," said he triumphantly, "under the rules o' the R-royal Humane Society, ye must give me hot whisky and water. Do not put temptation before the laddie. He's my nephew an' a good boy i' the main. Tho' why he should masquerade as Mister Thackeray on the high seas is beyond my comprehension. Oh, the vanity o' youth! McPhee told me you were as vain as a peacock. I mind that now."

There is no need here to follow the events through their procession to the seventh heaven of lunatic unexpectedness. Let us turn to the fact that the end of the tale is the revenge of the narrator on the man who had put him to so many side-splitting inconveniences. And this is worth noting, because the theme of most of Kipling's comic stories is the theme of revenge. This is particularly noticeable when a number of them are gathered in one volume, as in *Stalky & Co*. There is indeed a certain sameness in most of these stories to which the Rev. John Gillett draws attention when he says, in *The Impressionists:* "Every time that anyone has taken direct steps against No. 5 study, the issue has been more or less humiliating to the taker". As a matter of fact, five out of the nine stories are exemplifica-

The First Maturity

tions of this judgement. Neither Beresford's recollections, however, nor Kipling's suggest that any reprisals like these ever were carried out. These stories were, in modern jargon, "wish-fulfilments". Or, rather, they were what the mature writer made out of his recollections of wishes he had once desired to be fulfilled. It may be that all our fairy-stories originated in the mouths of Cinderellas and preternaturally gifted younger sons. But here we return to the argument that there is a certain fairy-story element in most of Kipling's work during the 'Nineties. He was trying, without getting away from ultimate truth, to make a picture of life as it is *and* as it should be in terms such as ordinary life does not provide. His most successful attempt to do this is to be found in the two *Jungle Books*.

The germ of Mowgli is to be found in *Beast and Man in India* where Lockwood Kipling writes: "India is probably the cradle of wolf-child stories, which are here universally believed and supported by a cloud of testimony, including, in the famous Lucknow case of a wolf-boy, the evidence of European witnesses". There have been other cases since and it may be taken as reasonably certain that children abandoned for one reason or another (generally for the same reason) in the Indian jungle are sometimes suckled by she-wolves. But there

Rudyard Kipling

are no Mowglis among them. They are, without exception, described as being (what indeed one might expect) brutish, with a brutishness which is duller and denser than that of the brutes themselves. They have lost their birthright in one world without acquiring a compensation in the other.

Mowgli, then, is the hero of a fairy-story, but of one of the great fairy-stories of the world. It is probable that if the hundreds of thousands of Kipling's readers were asked to vote for the saving of only one of his characters from destruction, Mowgli would head the list with a very handsome majority. Who is there who does not know what happened to Mowgli and why should I, save for the sheer pleasure of it, recount it here?

His parents, the woodcutter and his wife, abandoned him when they were frightened by Shere Khan, the lame tiger. Mother Wolf, Raksha the Demon, suckled him and he was in due course presented to the Pack and accepted on the word of Baloo, the brown bear, and the gift of a bull from Bagheera, the black panther. Thus the stage is set and the characters are assembled for the fairy-tale, with the young hero and his friends and his mentors and the enemy with whom at last he must fight to the death.

It comes as a surprise to the statistically minded reader to find that there are, in all, only nine

The First Maturity

stories about Mowgli. One of these is of a different sort from the rest. It is *In the Rukh*, which was included in *Many Inventions*, a year before the first publication of the first *Jungle Book*. Here we find the wolf-boy already grown-up, determined to marry the daughter of a Forestry officer's fat Mohammedan butler. Mowgli is here made to appear decidedly uncanny but there is no real magic about him. He knows more about the beasts of the jungle than a man should know, but he is not shown in fairy-tale communion with them. Had Kipling written no more about him than this, we should have remembered *In the Rukh* as one remembers some score of stories that are only very good.

But from this tentative beginning Kipling characteristically went on to something that is much greater. Mowgli ceases to be only a fascinating exhibit in the great anthropological museum that (from one point of view) India is. He becomes a myth, like Brer Rabbit or the Centaur or Reynard the Fox. As I have said before, Kipling has the myth-making genius. It is rare in modern literature but it is a sign of greatness whenever it occurs — and to the extent to which it does occur. It is not always combined with the highest literary ability — Sherlock Holmes is a very good example of that — but when it is the combination is potent.

Rudyard Kipling

The best of all these stories is *Kaa's Hunting* in which we see Mowgli as the pupil and companion of Baloo and Bagheera but visibly approaching the end of his apprenticeship to the ways of the jungle. Baloo is the teacher of theory, and Bagheera the believer in action. Mowgli is the still unlicked cub, with plenty of good stuff in him, who has to learn not only from the precept and example of his friends but also from his own mistakes. When Baloo has finished boasting to Bagheera of what he has taught his charge, they suddenly find that Mowgli has been listening to the wayward and aimless seductions of the *Bandar-log*. Only a little while before the man-cub has been repeating his knowledge:

"Now for the Snake-People," said Bagheera.

The answer was a perfectly indescribable hiss, and Mowgli kicked up his feet behind, clapped his hands to applaud himself, and jumped on to Bagheera's back, where he sat sideways, drumming with his heels on the glossy skin and making the worst faces he could think of at Baloo.

"There — there! That was worth a little bruise," said the brown bear tenderly. "Some day thou wilt remember me." Then he turned aside to tell Bagheera how he had begged the Master Words from Hathi the Wild Elephant, who knows all about these things, and

The First Maturity

how Hathi had taken Mowgli down to a pool to get the Snake Word from a water-snake, because Baloo could not pronounce it, and how Mowgli was now reasonably safe against all accidents in the jungle, because neither snake, bird, nor beast would hurt him.

Then the man-cub's companions go to sleep and he is snatched away from between them and hurried across the tree-tops by the Monkey-People. Baloo and Bagheera know that the Monkey-People may forget and drop him at any moment — for to Kipling the *Bandar-log* are the symbol of conceit and planlessness.[1] Mowgli remembers to give "the Kite call for — 'We be of one blood, thou and I ' ", so that Chil the Kite is able to report to his friends. Kipling believes in the efficacy of sound instruction given to sound young material. Baloo and Bagheera wheedle Kaa, the great python, into joining their rescue party and they have to go slowly about their wheedling while time is slipping away. Kipling knows the value of suspense at the right moment. The three of them rescue Mowgli from the Monkey-People in a great battle in the deserted city, the Cold Lairs. Kipling knows how to use physical action for his climax.

---

[1]This made so deep an impression on the contemporary world that Mr. Wells imagined the word "*Bandar-log*" being used as a description of "the mob" two centuries after his own time.

Rudyard Kipling

When the battle is over Mowgli shows the sweetness of the sound young material that is in him:

"We be one blood, thou and I," Mowgli answered. "I take my life from thee tonight. My kill shall be thy kill if ever thou art hungry, O Kaa."

"All thanks, Little Brother," said Kaa, though his eyes twinkled. "And what may so bold a hunter kill? I ask that I may follow when next he goes abroad."

"I kill nothing — I am too little, — but I drive goats towards such as can use them. When thou art empty come to me and see if I speak the truth. I have some skill in these [he held out his hands], and if ever thou art in a trap, I may pay the debt which I owe to thee, to Bagheera, and to Baloo, here. Good hunting to ye all, my masters."

"Well said," growled Baloo, for Mowgli had returned thanks very prettily.

Then comes that cunningest trick of the great story-teller — the second climax, most effective, as here, when it is briefer, quieter and more mysterious than the first. Kaa hypnotises the monkeys, by dancing to them and it is only Mowgli, with his hands on their shoulders, who draws Baloo and Bagheera away from the dreadful fascination. The three go home together before Kaa has come to the end of his dance. But the story is even now not yet done, since Bagheera appeals to the Law of the Jungle:

The First Maturity

Baloo did not wish to bring Mowgli into any more trouble, but he could not tamper with the Law, so he mumbled: "Sorrow never stays punishment. But remember, Bagheera, he is very little."

"I will remember; but he has done mischief, and blows must be dealt now. Mowgli, hast thou anything to say?"

"Nothing. I did wrong. Baloo and thou are wounded. It is just."

Bagheera gave him half a dozen love-taps; from a panther's point of view they would hardly have waked one of his own cubs, but for a seven-year-old boy they amounted to as severe a beating as you could wish to avoid. When it was all over Mowgli sneezed, and picked himself up without a word.

The whole piece stands by the side of *The Man Who Would Be King*, when considered from the point of view of the excellence of its composition. But there is more to be said about it than that. Was there ever a medicinal draught that slid down the throat as easily or with a more delicious after-taste? For *Kaa's Hunting*, as I have tried to show, is, on one side of it, strictly medicinal. Almost the whole of Kipling's practical philosophy of life is easily deducible from it, and yet — it is one of the great short stories of the world, one of the most beautiful specimens of its author's art. It

Rudyard Kipling

was written while he still felt sure that he knew what medicine to prescribe.

IV

The main difficulty in dealing with the poetry which Kipling published during his first maturity is that it is a wilderness, containing a great deal of what is usually meant when the unthinking speak, whether in appreciation or in disapprobation, of what they consider to be characteristically "Kipling's poetry". Liking or disliking, too many of them are equally apt to be wrong. There is much in this considerable body of work which cannot be ranked high but which has an immediate, vigorous appeal and which has raised up a large crop of imitators. Kipling must be given all possible credit for having written it with so much effectiveness and for having provided a medium for such men of ability as "Banjo" Patterson in Australia, Mr. Robert W. Service in Canada and, in England, Mr. Patrick MacGill and Mr. Gilbert Frankau. There is, however, sound self-criticism in what he himself says of the famous reciter's piece about "mad Carew":

It was luscious and rampant, with a touch, I thought, of the suburban Toilet-Club school favoured by the late Mr. Oscar Wilde. Yet, and this to me was the

The First Maturity

Devil of it, it carried for one reader an awesome suggestion of "but for the Grace of God there goes Richard Baxter."

But we must be very careful before we are contemptuous of the style in which Kipling wrote, for example, *The Rhyme of the Three Sealers:*

Tom Hall stood up by the quarter-rail. "Your words in your teeth," said he,
"There's never a law of God or man runs north of Fifty-Three.
So go in grace with Him to face, and an ill-spent life behind,
And I'll be good to your widows, Rube, as many as I can find."
A *Stralsund* man shot blind and large, and a warlock Finn was he,
And he hit Tom Hall with a bursting ball a hand's-breadth over the knee.
Tom Hall caught hold by the topping-lift, and sat him down with an oath,
"You'll wait a little, Rube," he said, "the Devil has called for both.
The Devil is driving both this tide, and the killing-grounds are close,
And we'll go up to the Wrath of God, as the hollus-chickie goes."

It is first-rate stuff of its kind and Kipling taught the world how ramping, roaring verse of that

Rudyard Kipling

kind should be written. But some of those whom he taught have written it nearly as well as he could himself. If he had done nothing better in verse, it would not be possible to rank him so high as a poet as I shall attempt to do. There are, however, earlier lines, some of which I have quoted on earlier pages of this book, which entitle him to make a larger claim.

During the 'Nineties, he fully substantiated that claim. Some of the work with which he did so was written before he left India. Scraps of it, printed as mottoes for stories, showed that he was already making an enormous advance on *Departmental Ditties*, though, to be sure, he had done no more than redeem a promise which had been unequivocally made. But the advance was a mixed matter. Some of it was in the direction of *The Three Sealers* and *Gunga Din*, an appeal to the talents of the reciter. And some of it, which produced a still enduring confusion, looked on the surface as though it must be the same kind of stuff. It was written in the Cockney dialect of the private soldier, and why should a poet adopt that medium unless he wished to be either virile or pathetic in the manner of the reciter? It followed that a number of critics tended to class some of his first-rate work with what was only second-

The First Maturity

rate. But a good deal of his best work has been done in this medium, as in the time-expired man's reflections on the way home from India:

> Oh, I 'ave come upon the books,
>   An' frequent broke a barrick-rule,
> An' stood beside an' watched myself
>   Be'avin' like a bloomin' fool.
> I paid my price for findin' out,
>   Nor never grutched the price I paid,
> But sat in Clink without my boots,
>   Admirin' 'ow the world was made.
>
>   .   .   .   .
>
> My girl she said, "Oh, stay with me!"
>   My mother 'eld me to 'er breast.
> They've never written none, an' so
>   They must 'ave gone with all the rest —
> With all the rest which I 'ave seen
>   An' found an' known an' met along.
> I cannot say the things I feel
>   And so I sing my evenin' song:
>
> *For to admire an' for to see,*
>   *For to be'old this world so wide —*
> *It never done no good to me,*
>   *But I can't drop it if I tried!*

That is not mere reciter's stuff. Nor, for all its popularity in the mouths of baritones, is *Manda-*

Rudyard Kipling

lay, nor is *Danny Deever;* nor yet is *Ford o' Kabul River:*

>Kabul town's by Kabul river —
>Blow the bugle, draw the sword —
>There I lef' my mate for ever,
>   Wet an' drippin' by the ford.
>   Ford, ford, ford o' Kabul river,
>   Ford o' Kabul river in the dark!
>   There's the river up an' brimmin', an'
>   there's 'arf a squadron swimmin'
>   'Cross the ford o' Kabul river in the dark.
>
>Kabul town's a blasted place —
>Blow the bugle, draw the sword —
>'Strewth I shan't forget 'is face
>   Wet an' drippin' by the ford!
>   Ford, ford, ford o' Kabul river,
>   Ford o' Kabul river in the dark!
>   Keep the crossing-stakes beside you, an' they
>   will surely guide you
>   'Cross the ford o' Kabul river in the dark.

When he wrote these and a good many others in the same style Kipling qualified for a place among the English dialect-writers, who are few and far between. He took moreover for his medium a dialect which no one before him had ever suspected of being possible as a vehicle for poetry. It had been exploited for purposes both of humour and of pathos of the crudest sort. But he showed

The First Maturity

that it was capable of being used as a genuine poetic speech, flexible, and with a surprisingly wide range of tones. He knew the people of whom he was writing and his interpretation of their experiences gained, as he meant that it should do, from being uttered in their own language.

It is noteworthy, too, that the use of dialect seems often to have exercised a restraining influence on him. In poetry, his besetting sin, as it never was in prose, was a too flamboyant use of rhetoric. I do not mean that his rhetoric is not enjoyable. It is refreshing if only for the sheer, confident, swashbuckling swagger of it, and in invective he has often used it with magnificent force, as witness such poems as *Cleared* and *Gehazi*. But if Kipling had only these and the swinging metres of *Tomlinson* and *M'Andrew's Hymn* to recommend him we should be justified in concluding that as a prose-writer he would long outlive his own poetic reputation. Dialect taught him caution. He was on delicate ground where a false step would bring him in a moment into the merely grotesque or the merely crude. It was unexpected that a writer in Cockney should be restrained, where heartiness and exaggeration were almost prescribed by custom. It was so unexpected that by many the restraint went unnoticed. The Kipling whose bent it was to show us life by "flashes

Rudyard Kipling

of magnificent vulgarity" must surely be indulging in a carnival of vulgarity when he chose to write verse not even in the speech of poetic rustics but in that of the common people of the slums. But as time goes by we can see more clearly that in those pieces lies a fundamental part of his achievement and an irremovable addition to English literature. And perhaps here he learnt a lesson in reticence, in discreet and elusive statement, which was to bear other fruit later on.

But his rhetoric did serve another purpose besides those of swashbuckling and invective. I have already given my opinion of the widespread belief that he was disappointed and embittered because he was never made Poet Laureate. But it is not difficult to see how the belief grew up. He was in so many respects so obviously the man for the place. After Tennyson's death, no living poet, with the possible exception of Swinburne (who was in any case impossible) excelled him in the writing of verse, at once sonorous and epigrammatic, for great public occasions. There was a four years' interregnum after Tennyson's death and then the cynical Lord Salisbury appointed the ridiculous Alfred Austin. It was clearly useless to turn to Austin for a dignified expression of national feeling and so it was to Kipling that the nation turned instead. More

The First Maturity

often than not, he responded nobly. He never believed that public events were unfit material for poetry, since they did arouse his own deepest emotions. Sometimes he did make true poetry out of them, as in *Recessional*. Rarely did he fail to make admirable and eloquent verse, and he wrote more pieces of the sort that a Laureate ought to write than, perhaps, any Laureate who ever wore the crown. The climax of this fine verse (as distinguished from poetry) is to be found in *The Dead King*, which he composed for the death of Edward VII:

For to him, above all, was Life good, above all he commanded
  Her abundance full-handed.
The peculiar treasure of Kings was his for the taking.
All that men come to in dreams he inherited waking: —
His marvel of world-gathered armies — one heart and
  all races;
His seas 'neath his keels when his war-castles foamed to
  their places;
The thundering foreshores that answered his heralded
  landing;
The huge lighted cities adoring, the assemblies up-
  standing;
The Councils of Kings called in haste to learn how he
  was minded —
The Kingdoms, the Powers and the Glories he dealt
  with unblinded.

Rudyard Kipling

This is the rhetoric of a master and we need not pause to examine its historical truth. It is a hymn to monarchy as a symbol — and since our disposition is to hold firmly to that symbol, it is as well that one of our poets should have celebrated it in such verse as this. The piece makes an odd contrast with the thin, shrill pipings that commemorated the death of George V, only a few days after Kipling's own. Not ill was it said at the time that "the King has gone and taken his trumpeter with him".

CHAPTER V

The Prophet of Empire in Defeat

THE SOUTH AFRICAN WAR was a crucial event in Kipling's life, and it may be described as the watershed between his second period and the third. We are apt today a little to underestimate the effect of this war on British opinion at the time. We think in terms of the War of 1914 and that, considered from the point of view of sheer statistics, appears to make the earlier conflict look a trifle foolish. It is difficult to imagine now how the public could have been as shocked as it was by our losses at Magersfontein and the Tugela, when we think of the Somme and Passchendaele. The successful defence of Mafeking was not quite so important a matter as the fall of Kut. We sent some quarter of a million men to South Africa — a mere side-show by the standards of 1914–1918.

But to take this point of view is in reality to

see the affair in a false proportion. In South Africa we were sustaining a military effort, at a distance of thousands of miles, on a scale which we had never attempted before. We had not an ally in the world, and were far from feeling that we had even any friends. We were sending the best of our fighting material over a route which could be cut the moment we lost command of the sea. And, in the hard practical world, we had no alternative but to take the immense risks that we did. Fate summoned the British Empire to prove that its greatness was not hollow and, even if our statesmen had desired to evade the challenge, there was no evasion open to them. The Dutch Republics had recovered their independence already and they aspired — as why should they not? — to bring the whole of South Africa under Dutch rule. They knew, indeed, that, unless they could do that, their whole way of life must be undermined by the influence which, coming from the South, had lapped round them in Rhodesia and Bechuanaland and had established a dangerous base of power in their very midst at Johannesburg.

For them it was now or never; it was their last chance. They considered that it was at least a sporting chance. They calculated, reasoning from previous experience, that initial reverses

The Prophet of Empire in Defeat

would make the British Cabinet think more than twice before taking the risks all over the world which an adequate military effort would entail. And for just that reason the British Cabinet had no choice but to make every effort that was required. To have done anything else would have been an admission of fear to do so that might have had cataclysmic results.

It was a tragic issue, and for Kipling a painful, perplexing and anxious issue. He regarded the British Empire, as did his friend, Cecil Rhodes, as the main instrument of civilisation then active in the world. The ideas of the two men were very much the same — and no one who has studied the career of Cecil Rhodes will believe that he pursued money, or even power, for selfish ends alone. Kipling, for his part, believed every word that in this year of 1899 he wrote in *The White Man's Burden:*

> Take up the White Man's burden —
>   Send forth the best ye breed —
> Go bind your sons to exile
>   To serve your captives' need;
> To wait in heavy harness,
>   On fluttered folk and wild —
> Your new-caught, sullen peoples,
>   Half-devil and half-child.

. . . .

Rudyard Kipling

> Take up the White Man's burden —
> The savage wars of peace —
> Fill full the mouth of Famine
> And bid the sickness cease;
> And when your goal is nearest
> The end for others sought,
> Watch Sloth and heathen Folly
> Bring all your hope to nought.

That, he believed with a Biblical fervour, was the appointed work of the British Empire, and in the last resort he held that the Empire would be justified in any action necessary to preserve its power to do that work.

There could be no doubt as to his acquiescence in the view that the war was necessary. But it was equally certain that he could not feel happy about it. He had a considerable liking for the Boers and a sympathy with their way of life. He knew as well as any man that we did not go into the field with entirely clean hands, and that there were scoundrels as well as patriots who desired the British cause to prevail. Further, he could not be sure that in this test, which seemed as though it had indeed been arranged by a conscious Fate, the forces of the Empire would assert themselves with the efficiency of which he had dreamed. He had spent a good deal of his time since he left India in learning how things were done with us.

The Prophet of Empire in Defeat

Politicians who were not afraid to fight were better than politicians who were, but they were still politicians. Perhaps he still put his trust in the soldiers; perhaps even there he had his misgivings.

We find an appropriate reflection of his state of mind in the extraordinarily obscure poem, *The Old Issue*, with which he greeted the outbreak of the war. It is so obscure that any reader might be pardoned for thinking at first that it was meant as an encouragement to the Boers to resist. It begins with:

"Here is nothing new nor aught unproven," say the
 Trumpets,
"Many feet have worn it and the road is old indeed.
It is the King – the King we schooled aforetime!"
(Trumpets in the marshes – in the eyot at Runny-
 mede!)

"Here is neither haste, nor hate, nor anger," peal the
 Trumpets,
"Pardon for his penitence or pity for his fall.
"It is the King!" – inexorable Trumpets –
(Trumpets round the scaffold at the dawning by
 Whitehall!)

Surely an incitement to the Republics to defend themselves against the aggression of the English Crown? But as one reads on with puzzled eyes,

Rudyard Kipling

it begins to be possible to see what is the case that Kipling is trying to make:

Howso' great the clamour, whatsoe'er their claim,
Suffer not the old King under any name!

*Here is naught unproven — here is naught to learn.
It is written what shall fall if the King return.*

He shall mark our goings, question whence we came,
Set his guards about us, as in Freedom's name.

He shall take a tribute; toll of all our ware;
He shall change our gold for arms — arms we may not bear.

He shall break his Judges if they cross his word;
He shall rule above the Law calling on the Lord.

He shall peep and mutter; and the night shall bring
Watchers 'neath our window, lest we mock the King —

Hate and all division; hosts of hurrying spies;
Money poured in secret, carrion breeding flies.

Strangers of his counsel, hirelings of his pay,
These shall deal our Justice; sell — deny — delay.

We shall drink dishonour, we shall eat abuse
For the Land we look to — for the Tongue we use.

The Prophet of Empire in Defeat

He is speaking of the Uitlanders in Johannesburg and his poem does not differ in essence, only in discretion and artistic skill, from the foolish poem which Alfred Austin had written three years earlier on the Jameson Raid. The issue in South Africa was deeper and, in the last analysis, cleaner than the struggle of the Uitlanders for the fine old English liberties which the unruly barons asserted at Runnymede and the rich Puritans on the scaffold in Whitehall. But Kipling hardly attempted to make that clear. Incidentally, he omitted to notice that both John and Charles I did try, though each was doomed to failure by circumstances and his own limitations, to realise his own ideal of the "strong man ruling alone".

It is particularly important to observe that after this Kipling made no further attempt to argue the merits of the case. He did not renew and re-renew polemic, as he did against Germany between 1914 and 1918. His most popular poem of the time was *The Absent-minded Beggar*, of which he is reported to have said that, if it had not meant committing suicide, he would have liked to kill the author. For a long time he would not, for perfectly comprehensible reasons, reprint it. It was a thing which had served its purpose and might be forgotten. When at last he did include it among his collected poems a generation which but

Rudyard Kipling

dimly remembered it was able to judge how well it had served its purpose, and, whatever its demerits, how much more worthy of its author it was than *The Old Issue*. It was written to raise money for the families of the men who were fighting in South Africa. It had a taking lilt and was full of phrases which clung to the memory like burrs. It came with full sincerity out of the heart of a man who had always fought for better treatment for the Army and who had already written:

I went into a public-'ouse to get a pint o' beer,
The publican 'e up an' sez, "We serve no red-coats here."
The girls be'ind the bar they laughed and giggled fit to die,
I outs into the street again an' to myself sez I:
    O it's Tommy this, an' Tommy that, an' "Tommy, go away,"
    But it's "Thank you, Mister Atkins," when the band begins to play —
    The band begins to play, my boy, the band begins to play,
    O it's "Thank you, Mister Atkins," when the band begins to play.

The Absent-minded Beggar was an immense success and Kipling became one of the earliest heroes of a war which everyone but a few wise men

The Prophet of Empire in Defeat

supposed would not be much more than a brilliant military promenade.

He was, I think, one of these wise men. Certainly at no time did he say anything to encourage an easy optimism. He did not waste any more time over making a case against the enemy. He displayed no amazed horror over our early defeats. He did not relieve his feelings by "Killing Kruger wiv 'is mouf". He did not even celebrate our victories when at last we began to win them. The English world might go "mafficking" on Mafeking Night but Kipling did not go with it. His was another task. He went to South Africa himself and spent some time as near to the fighting as he could get, part of it occupied at Bloemfontein in editing a paper for the troops. His main function was to observe what happened and to draw such morals as he could.

His themes, then, turned out to be two — the heroism, sufferings and good humour of the men and the regimental officers, and the ill-handling in higher places which had wasted so many lives and so much time and had so greatly increased the risk to the Empire which the whole affair involved. His rough conclusions on both he put into the mouth of the "English Lord" to whom Laughton O. Zigler had an introduction, in *The Captive*, and who said that "the British soldier had failed in every

Rudyard Kipling

point except courage". Several years afterwards, in a speech made to schoolboys, he gave a vivid little glimpse of his own experience:

> I happened to be in Bloemfontein after a "regrettable incident" called Sanna's Post — where we lost five or six hundred men and several guns in a little ambush. I met one of the survivors a few hours after the thing had happened. He had done very well in a losing game, and he had come out of it, looking exactly like a man after the last half of a really hectic footer game. His clothes were ripped to bits, but his temper was quite good. After he'd told his tale I said to him: "What are we going to do about it?" He said: "Oh, I don't know. 'Thank Heaven we have within the land five hundred as good as they' ".

The war, as he could not help seeing, was a mess, a lamentable mess in which the news of affairs like that of Sanna's Post was dreaded at headquarters every day. But there was an enormous consolation in the spirit of the individual soldier, such as the man who thus jauntily quoted *Chevy Chase* in the moment of humiliating disaster. There were other consolations to which I shall come in a moment. But the heart of what he saw is in a handful of poems of pure description, and the best of these is that extraordinary piece called *Boots*, a feat of technical virtuosity which even Kipling, virtuoso as he was in the

The Prophet of Empire in Defeat

handling of rhythms, never surpassed. It is perhaps wrong to quote a few lines since the full effect depends on the complete thirty-two, with those subtle variations in monotony which make monotony only more overwhelming. But the temptation is not to be resisted:

Don't — don't — don't — don't — look at what's in front of you.
(Boots — boots — boots — boots — movin' up an' down again);
Men — men — men — men — men go mad with watchin' 'em,
    An' there's no discharge in the war!

Try — try — try — try — to think o' something different —
Oh — my — God — keep — me from goin' lunatic!
(Boots — boots — boots — boots — movin' up an' down again!)
    There's no discharge in the war!

It conveys the feeling of tired men on the march with an exactness beyond praise. And it is perhaps the most remarkable of all the many examples of Kipling's peculiar gift of *physical* sympathy, of rendering, with as much poignancy as though he had experienced them himself, physical sensations which had been only described to him.

One of the consolations which the war gave to

Rudyard Kipling

him was no doubt a good deal more important from his point of view than the ultimate victory. He had seen the virtues in action not only of his old friends, the Regulars, educated for years for this work, but also of the raw stuff out from England, men who hitherto had never even dreamed of a soldier's life. He makes his General in *The Captive* say to the captured Boer commandant:

"Was there anything wrong with the men who upset Van Besters' apple-cart last month when he was trying to cross the line to join Piper with those horses he'd stole from Gabbitas?"

"No, General," says Van Zyl. "Your men got the horses back and eleven dead; and Van Besters, he ran to Delarey in his shirt. They was very good, those men. They shoot hard."

"*So* pleased to hear you say so. I laid 'em down at the beginning of this century — a 1900 vintage. You remember 'em, Mankletow?" he says. "The Central Middlesex Broncho Busters — clerks and floor-walkers mostly," and he wiped his moustache.

The stuff was good and there was reason to hope that, as it had withstood this unexpectedly severe trial, so it would withstand the severer trial which Kipling foresaw. As indeed it did — this passage is simply a forecast of Kitchener's Armies. There was another consolation in the presence and usefulness of the men of the Empire

The Prophet of Empire in Defeat

to whom he paid tribute in that charming little poem about the New South Wales Contingent:

> Smells are surer than sounds or sights
>   To make your heart-strings crack —
> They start those awful voices o' nights
>   That whisper, "Old man, come back!"
> That must be why the big things pass
>   And the little things remain,
> Like the smell of the wattle by Lichtenberg,
>   Riding in, in the rain.
>
>   .   .   .   .
>
> I have forgotten a hundred fights,
>   But one I shall not forget —
> With the raindrops bunging up my sights
>   And my eyes bunged up with wet;
> And through the crack and stink of the cordite
>   (Ah Christ! My country again!)
> The smell of the wattle by Lichtenberg,
>   Riding in, in the rain!

But that was all there was to be put on the credit side of the account, and there was a terrifying amount to be put on the other. The early operations of the war revealed only too plainly an army that might be efficient in its smallest units and in most of its individuals but that was, beyond any argument, grossly inefficient as a whole. We had accepted a heavy and dangerous task and the men in the higher places had made it ten times as

Rudyard Kipling

heavy and ten times as dangerous as it need have been. Nor were these men in the higher places "the politicians" whom soldiers always blame and whom Kipling was disposed to distrust. They were the leaders of the troops in the field:

The General got 'is decorations thick
  (The men that backed 'is lies could not complain)
The Staff 'ad D.S.O.'s till we was sick,
  An' the soldier — 'ad the work to do again!
For 'e might 'ave known the District was an 'otbed,
  Instead of 'andin' over, upside-down,
To a man 'oo 'ad to fight 'alf a year to put it right,
  While the General went an' slandered 'im in town!

> An' it all went into the laundry,
> But it never came out in the wash.
> We were sugared about by the old men
> (Panicky, perishin' old men)
> That 'amper an' 'inder an' scold men
> For fear o' Stellenbosch![1]

An embittered regimental officer in 1917 and 1918 would have expressed himself precisely thus.

In earlier days Kipling had written in breezy language his conception of the civilising mission of the British:

The 'eathen in 'is blindness bows down to wood an'
  stone;

---

[1] Stellenbosch was the town where unsuccessful Generals went to be, in the expression of a later war, *dégommés*.

The Prophet of Empire in Defeat

'E don't obey no orders unless they is 'is own;
'E keeps 'is side-arms awful: 'e leaves 'em all about,
An' then comes up the Regiment an' pokes the heathen out.
All along o' dirtiness, all along o' mess,
All along o' doin' things rather-more-or-less. . . .

It was now to be retorted against him, and with justice, that in the larger sense the British Army had kept its side-arms pretty awful and that dirtiness, mess and the habit of doing things rather more or less had exposed us to the ridicule or the pity of the world — and perhaps to its cupidity as well. It was true that the war had been brought to a victorious close, that the beleaguered towns had been relieved, the enemy defeated in the field, and the territories of the two Republics incorporated in the Empire. But it was a triumph in which there were few who could take any pride save the members of the rank and file, who knew that they had done what had been done in spite of their leaders. It was like what sometimes happens in an Association Football Cup Tie, when a first-class team only just struggles home by the odd goal, after being down at half-time, against a little team from nowhere in particular. It was one of those victories which call for as much heart-searching as any defeat.

Kipling faced the facts and admitted as much.

Rudyard Kipling

It is significant, as I have remarked, that he did not celebrate in verse any of our victories, not even the reliefs of Ladysmith, Kimberley and Mafeking. His last word on the South African War was a poem which was famous at the time, in which he said: "We have had a jolly good lesson and it serves us jolly well right". He went on:

It was our fault, and our very great fault — and now we must turn it to use.
We have forty million reasons for failure, but not a single excuse.
So the more we work and the less we talk the better results we shall get —
We have had an Imperial lesson; it may make us an Empire yet!

Perhaps the best comment ever made on that note of hopefulness was made by himself many years afterwards, when in his collected verse he placed next to it the poem he wrote in 1917 on the report of the Royal Commission which investigated the scandals of the Mesopotamian Campaign:

Our dead shall not return to us while Day and Night divide —
  Never while the bars of sunset hold.
But the idle-minded overlings who quibbled while they died,
  Shall they thrust for high employment as of old?

The Prophet of Empire in Defeat

Shall we only threaten and be angry for an hour?
   When the storm is ended shall we find
How softly but how swiftly they have sidled back to
    power
   By the favour and contrivance of their kind?

This juxtaposition of the two pieces seems to say, as plainly as Kipling can speak: "The answer is probably 'Yes' — at any rate to judge from our experience after the South African War". It did not take him until 1917 to see that his optimism of 1902 was ill-founded. The succeeding years were much taken up with the question of Army Reform and Kipling was in a good position to know what progress was being made and what the difficulties were. He gave his opinion in *The Song of the Old Guard:*

> "Know this, my brethren, Heaven is clear
>   And all the clouds are gone —
> The Proper Sort shall flourish now,
>   Good times are coming on" —
> The evil that was threatened late
>   To all of our degree,
> Hath passed in discord and debate,
>   And, *Hey then up go we!*
>
>   .   .   .   .
>
> Our altars which the heathen brake
>   Shall rankly smoke anew,

Rudyard Kipling

And anise, mint and cummin take
  Their dread and sovereign due,
Whereby the buttons of our trade
  Shall soon restorèd be
With curious work in gilt and braid,
  And, *Hey then up go we!*

Then come, my brethren, and prepare
  The candlesticks and bells,
The scarlet, brass, and badger's hair
  Wherein our Honour dwells,
And straitly fence and strictly keep
  The Ark's integrity
Till Armageddon break our sleep. . . .
  And, *Hey then up go we!*

It was a bitter judgement but is there anyone who would dare, in the light of the years between 1914 and 1918, to say that it was false?

Long before 1914 Kipling was fully conscious that we had learnt next to nothing from the "Imperial lesson" that the Boers had given us. Probably his experiences in South Africa had given him a sick foreboding that we never should. The South African War was a crucial period in his life because it brought about in him that change of mind which often comes over men of ideals who are also realists. He did not abandon his ideals. He continued to believe that civilisation,

The Prophet of Empire in Defeat

and only civilisation, can set free the soul of man, because it alone can deliver him from the fear of plague and famine. He continued to believe that those who could see civilisation in this light had received a mission to spread it. But in spite of one or two brave utterances he ceased to believe with the old fervour that the British people could, or at any rate would, carry out this mission.

To this extent he was hereafter a disillusioned man. His disillusionment shows in such poems as *The Islanders* and *The City of Brass*, in which he reviled the weaknesses of the British people with all the magnificent forces of rhetoric at his command. But he had the greatness of mind to endure disillusionment without becoming embittered. Much of what had fed his soul up to now had been taken from him or had changed its flavour, but he found new sources of nourishment. He made himself again and in so doing entered into a new and a finer phase as an artist.

And for him the need for heart-searching was particularly acute, since he had led the British people to expect something very different. He had written:

"India's full of Stalkies — Cheltenham and Haileybury and Marlborough chaps — that we don't know anything about, and the surprises will begin when there is really a big row on."

Rudyard Kipling

"Who will be surprised?" said Dick Four.

"The other side. The gentlemen who go to the front in first-class carriages. Just imagine Stalky let loose on the south side of Europe with a sufficiency of Sikhs and a reasonable prospect of loot. Consider it quietly."

"There's something in that, but you're too much of an optimist, Beetle," said the Infant.

He was — in the 'Nineties. The conditions were not exactly fulfilled. The big row did not occur on the south side and the Sikhs were not allowed to take part in it. But it was obvious either that the Stalkies were not forthcoming, or else that they were smothered by the inefficiency of the system. Kipling lost his optimism and did not regain it. It cannot have surprised him when in 1914 the Stalkies of that time were sent into action armed with swords and distinctively dressed so that they might be the more easily picked off by the enemy.

CHAPTER VI

The Golden Years

T<small>HE DIVISION</small> of an author's work into "periods" is as ticklish an undertaking as the division of the works of all mankind. The most formal historian nowadays observes an extreme caution when he uses the terms "ancient", "mediaeval" and "modern", and protects himself against the more literal forms of misunderstanding by every qualification he can think of. He knows that a man or an institution, plainly in character what we mean by "modern", is always likely to turn up in the ancient or the mediaeval world. Nevertheless we do mean something recognisable when we use these terms.

So it is with the work of authors and with Kipling's work, perhaps, more than with most. If we do not make our distinctions with delicacy and many reservations we shall find that we are

Rudyard Kipling

carving up a live body which writhes and refuses to submit. But the two divisions I have made so far — up to his final farewell to India and then from there up to the outbreak of the Boer War — seem to me to correspond roughly to realities. There are pieces in each period which do appear to belong in spirit more properly to the other — apart from the occasional difficulty of knowing to which period a given piece does actually belong in time. Kipling's whole life is full of harkings back and harkings forward, of which I have already given some examples. But there are substantial characteristics of the main body of work in each which justify the division. And I suggest (I dare not put it more strongly that that) that the events here named as dividing marks were of sufficient importance in Kipling's life to justify the prominence thus given to them.

That they alone account for the observable changes in his work it would be more than foolish even to attempt to maintain. You may say as well that he left India because a change was ripening with him as the converse. And I am assuredly not going to argue that the second change would not have happened if there had been no South African War or if it had gone otherwise. I do think, however, that the war and its lessons strongly helped a change that, again, was already

The Golden Years

ripening within him. Another way of looking at the facts and their consequences would be to say that his first maturity began when he left India to discover the world and his second when he came home from the world to discover England. Towards the end of the century his love of wandering showed signs of growing less. After an ill-fated attempt to settle in Torquay, in 1896 he took a house in Rottingdean. This village, though not then the roaring thoroughfare for cars and motor-coaches which it has since become, was near enough to Brighton to allow far too many sightseers to make a pilgrimage in the hope of catching a glimpse of a man who had never liked being looked at. A little later he moved to Burwash which even today is reasonably quiet and remote. But events prevented him from settling there in peace until the new century. Then he began to discover England there.

I have already said that India is a parish and that Kipling, when he left India, was in some danger of becoming parochial. But the world is a parish too. The cosmopolitan with no true roots in any one country tends to become as narrow as the man who never moves out of the village where he was born. Kipling (or rather his mother) asked: "What do they know of England who only England know?" But he came to realise

Rudyard Kipling

that the Englishman who wants to know the world ought to know his own country as well. When he first returned from India, however, he seemed hardly to know that it existed. There is something significant in his confession that during those early days in London:

> I was so ignorant, I never guessed when the great fogs fell that trains could take me to light and sunshine a few miles outside London. Once I faced the reflection of my own face in the jet-black mirror of the window-panes for five days.

It was not ignorance, of course. It was indifference. Even the years in Devonshire had left behind them no affection for English fields and hedgerows. That was to grow later.

I think, too, that he tried to express the meaning of the change that had occurred in him and the moment when he became conscious of it by placing the poem I am going to quote immediately before a group of some of the best pieces he wrote about England. It is placed in the mouth of an ex-Service man returning from South Africa:

> So 'ath it come to me — not pride,
>   Nor yet conceit, but on the 'ole
> (If such a term may be applied)
>   The makin's of a blooming soul.

The Golden Years

> But now, discharged, I fall away
>   To do with little things again. . . .
> Gawd, 'oo knows all I cannot say,
>   Look after me in Thamesfontein!

If England was what England seems,
And not the England of our dreams,
But only putty, brass an' paint,
'Ow quick we'd chuck 'er! But she ain't!

Some critics have picked on the last four of these lines as proof that his loudly expressed patriotism is only superficial or at best selfish. I cannot see any ground for the charge. One loves one's country for what she is, not as an abstraction. But in any case Kipling was now on his way to discover an England which was not all putty, brass and paint.

He himself has described the process of his "recall". The story called *An Habitation Enforced* can be profitably compared with another, *An Error in the Fouth Dimension*. In the earlier of the two, Wilton Sargent, a young American millionaire, sets out "with the versatility of his race ... to be just a little more English than the English". To this end he does a number of things, which are described in a slightly patronising manner (it is one of Kipling's less amiable stories) and, though not even his butler can break him of the habit of asking for "the Worcestershire sauce", he succeeds

Rudyard Kipling

in producing a very creditable imitation of the real thing. The imitation breaks down when Wilton "flags" and "boards" an important express which passes the end of his garden — as he would have done in his own country had he thought the occasion of sufficient importance. The railway company is unable to understand him or he it, and the end of the imbroglio is that he flees back to America, with every intention of staying there. It is perhaps a little trivial to seek an implication in what is after all only a gay and trivial piece of farce. But if there is an implication to be found, it is that Americans should not try to turn themselves back into Englishmen. The process they have already undergone is irreversible if there is anything in what the story says of Wilton when he begins to grow excited:

> There was no chance now of mistaking the man's nationality. Speech, gesture, and step, so carefully drilled into him, had gone away with the borrowed mask of indifference. It was a lawful son of the Youngest People, whose predecessors were the Red Indian. His voice had risen to the high, throaty crow of his breed when they labour under excitement.

George Chapin, in *An Habitation Enforced*, comes from the same world as Wilton Sargent — the world of American big business. But he has

The Golden Years

worked there until his nerves have given way. He and his wife drift, bored and aimless, about Europe, hating the life they are leading but not daring, for fear of George's life and sanity, to return to their own country. At last they meet a wise woman who sends them to stay at Rocketts, "the farm of one Cloke, in the southern counties — where, she assured them, they would meet the genuine England of folklore and song".

On their first morning, George wants to know where the nearest telegraph office is and they are given a line across country:

"No roads, no nothing!" said Sophie, her short skirt hooked by briers. "I thought all England was a garden. There's your spire, George, across the valley. How curious!"

They walked toward it through an all-abandoned land. Here they found the ghost of a patch of lucerne that had refused to die; there a harsh fallow surrendered to yard-high thistles; and here a breadth of rampant kelk feigning to be lawful crop. In the ungrazed pastures swaths of dead stuff caught their feet, and the ground beneath glistered with sweat. At the bottom of the valley a little brook had undermined its footbridge and frothed in the wreckage. But there stood great woods on the slopes beyond — old, tall, and brilliant, like unfaded tapestries against the wall of a ruined house.

Rudyard Kipling

It is to an abandoned house that, when they have been thus prepared, their walk leads them. The old shepherd who invites them to walk over it says proudly of the staircase, "Plenty room here for your coffin to come down. Seven foot and three men at each end wouldn't brish the paint." By an exquisite stroke of invention it is Sophie Chapin's discovery of this old man peacefully dead in the old farm at the back and her watching beside him which make the purchase of the house seem right to her. When George suggests that her experience may have put her against the plan, she exclaims, "No! What happened this morning seemed to be more of a — of a leading than anything else".

Now I am not concerned here to praise this lovely story in detail, nor have I cited it by way of proof that Kipling contradicts the implications of *An Error in the Fourth Dimension*. He is hardly to be taken as preaching that all Americans should buy properties in England and turn themselves into Englishmen again. The real point of the story is that it is as personal as a lyric, that it is a sincere and beautiful projection in the form of the short story of the author's own emotions. Kipling was not an American or a millionaire, he was not gathered in in just this way by the magic of the

The Golden Years

English countryside. But it is substantially true to say that until the beginning of the century England was not his home. He had no roots here. This is reflected in the consciousness one cannot escape after reading *An Habitation Enforced* that English landscapes have been exceedingly rare in his earlier work. There are some incidental schoolboy memories in *Stalky & Co.* There is a marvellous bravura piece of impressionism in *My Sunday at Home.* In *The Brushwood Boy* there are softer landscapes which, as we learn to expect with Kipling, seem to reach forward to his work in the next decade, and here perhaps we can best see the beginning of the fascination which was to grow until it became unescapable.

But *An Habitation Enforced* is the hymn of praise of the man who knows that he has come home and who knows also, in some mystical manner, that his return has been accepted and approved. Kipling at this time was in a peculiarly sensitive condition. On the private side of his life he had not long since suffered a grievous loss in the death of a dearly loved child. On the public side of his life he had received a grievous blow, not in the destruction of his political ideals but in a weakening of his confidence that they

Rudyard Kipling

could be realised. England now gave him not merely consolation but a new extension of life. Whereas on his departure from India he had sought this extension in space, he now found it in time.

In his manner (and this is a trick of his on which comment has not often been made) he attached to *An Habitation Enforced* a poem in which, in different terms and the different medium of verse, he says the same thing over again. This, though it is one of the best things he ever wrote, even considered in the company of what he did in his best period as a poet, does not excel its companion story in poignancy. But it must be quoted, if only for one phrase:

> I am the land of their fathers.
> In me the virtue stays.
> I will bring back my children,
> After certain days.
>
> Under their feet in the grasses
> My clinging magic runs.
> They shall return as strangers,
> They shall remain as sons.
>
> Over their heads in the branches
> Of their new-bought, ancient trees,
> I weave an incantation
> And draw them to my knees.

The Golden Years

Scent of smoke in the evening,
Smell of rain in the night —
The hours, the days and the seasons
Order their souls aright,

Till I make plain the meaning
Of all my thousand years —
Till I fill their hearts with knowledge,
While I fill their eyes with tears.

"All my thousand years!" It is to this feeling of the past that Kipling returns again and again throughout the work of his golden years. The English may make mistakes at home and abroad, the affairs of the Empire may go awry, but England is a country which has been built up by the work of generation after generation. She is not merely putty, brass and paint.

There are three other stories which, for the sense they show of the age-long tradition of the countryside, can be compared with *An Habitation Enforced*. They are *Friendly Brook*, *The Wish House* and, perhaps in a lesser degree, *My Son's Wife*. This last is, in a sense, a variation on the original theme. Frankwell Midmore takes to the country as a refuge, not from American big business, but from a sort of blood-curdling pre-War vision of post-War Bloomsbury. An aunt dies

Rudyard Kipling

and leaves him a little estate, on which he thus reports:

So far as I can understand, she has left me between four and five hundred a year. It all comes from Ther Land, as they call it down here. The unspeakable attorney, Sperrit, and a green-eyed daughter, who hums to herself as she tramps but is silent on all subjects except "huntin' ", insisted on taking me to see it. Ther Land is brown and green in alternate slabs like chocolate and pistachio cakes, speckled with occasional peasants who do not alter. In case it should not be wet enough there is a wet brook in the middle of it. Ther House is by the brook.

The design of the tale is not over-subtle. A disappointment in love drives Frankwell to the country to live in the house he has despised. Gradually he falls in love with what he finds. He grows more and more fascinated by the difficulties of this unfamiliar setting. He reads Jorrocks and painfully learns to ride. Inevitably he falls in love with the solicitor's green-eyed daughter. All this is less excellent than the ravishment and entanglement of George and Sophie Chapin. But the core of the story is in Sidney the farmer, with his pig-pound and his women ("Lor, *no*! The Sidneys don't marry. They keep. That's his fourth since — to my knowledge. He was a takin' man from the first"), and the flood which swirls into Frank-

The Golden Years

well's house and which Sidney cantankerously defies.

Friendly Brook is more of a piece, purely a story of the country. Jim Wickenden has adopted a daughter from "one o' those Lunnon Childern Societies". By the time Jim has become unalterably devoted to the child, the rapscallion father arrives to assert his rights. Jim pays him to go away and goes on paying him more and more until he is at his wit's end. And then one night the drunken blackmailer falls into the swollen brook and is drowned. That is why, to go back to the beginning of the story, Jim Wickenden refuses to move his stack out of the reach of a flood and says, "The Brook's been a good friend to me, an' if she's minded to have a snatch at my hay, *I* ain't settin' out to withstand her".

This little anecdote (as Kipling's critics would have called it in his earlier days) is told entirely in a conversation between two men who are trimming a field-hedge. From the sheer technical point of view, this story is a superb example of the way in which Kipling made every element in his material serve every other. It has been said that the means of a man of genius are ends in themselves, and here the strict analyst is hard put to it to make any distinction between means and ends. Is the anecdote for the sake of the two men in whose

Rudyard Kipling

conversation we are allowed to overhear it? Or is the kernel of the author's intention to be found in Jim Wickenden's pagan willingness to sacrifice his hay to the brook? It does not greatly matter. These different elements unite to make a story which only a deliberately assumed and unserviceable persistence in analysis could split into its component parts. We must take it as a picture which has its own organic, unarguable reasons for existing. But some hint of the reasons may be seen in a quotation:

They stood back and took stock of the neglected growth, tapped an elbow of hedge-oak here, a mossed beech-stub there, swayed a stooled ash back and forth, and looked at each other.

"I reckon she's about two rod thick," said Jabez the younger, "an' she hasn't felt iron since — when has she, Jesse?"

"Call it twenty-five year, Jabez, an' you won't be far out."

"Ummm!" Jabez rubbed his wet handbill on his wetter coat-sleeve. "She ain't a hedge. She's all manner o' trees. We'll just about have to——" He paused, as professional etiquette required.

"Just about have to side her up an' see what she'll bear. But hadn't we best——?" Jesse paused in his turn, both men being artists and equals.

"Get some kind o' line to go by." Jabez ranged up and down till he found a thinner place, and with clean

The Golden Years

snicks of the handbill revealed the original face of the fence. Jesse took over the dripping stuff as it fell forward, and, with a grasp and a kick, made it to lie orderly on the bank till it should be faggoted.

By noon a length of unclean jungle had turned itself into a cattle-proof barrier, tufted here and there with little plumes of the sacred holly which no woodman touches without orders.

Notice, in passing, Kipling's unsubdued delight in the power of the expert, with his technique, to bring order out of chaos.

The scene of *The Wish House* shifts and, though it is still noticeable, is only lightly sketched in. It is again, however, a story told through the conversation of two persons and again it is a story which has more than one aspect. Under one of them it might be classified among those tales of the borderland and beyond which I shall have to describe in another place. Mrs. Ashcroft, for the sake of the man she loves and who has left her, goes to the "Wish House" (which is, by an incomparable stroke, an empty house in a suburban street), rings the bell and says through the letter-box to "the Token" which dwells there: "Let me take everythin' bad, that's in store for my man, 'Arry Mockler, for love's sake". But Mrs. Fettley helps to draw out the story not merely of how the charm worked, but also of Mrs. Ashcroft's whole life. Both old ladies have lived their lives and look with stoicism towards the end, which already for Mrs. Ashcroft has shown itself above the horizon:

"It *do* 'urt sometimes. You shall see it when Nurse comes. She thinks I don't know it's turned."
Mrs. Fettley understood. Human nature seldom walks up to the word "cancer".

There are several hints here of the path which Kipling's genius was opening into the future. Even before this he had begun to concern himself more and more with the abnormal, both on the physical and on the spiritual plane. That is a matter which will recur later. For the moment I find myself most inclined to look back to a much earlier story on which comment has already been made in these pages — to *"Love o' Women"*. Mrs. Ashcroft is the feminine counterpart of Larry Tighe, but her portrait is painted by a much greater artist. There are no adventitious trappings of romance about her. Larry, be it remembered, was a gentleman-ranker. She is a village woman, whose whole life is spent in domestic service, with interludes of hopping. But she acts before us the part of a great lover with a convincingness which he never came near attaining. The Kipling of *"Love o' Women"* was, compared with the Kipling

The Golden Years

of *The Wish House*, no more than a very brilliant and original faker. It was his return to England, his passionate absorption in the stuff of England and the English people, which carried him over the gulf between the two.

II

But the new spirit in Kipling, the new light which glows in his work, is to be found not only in the stories he wrote about England, but also in his supreme story of Indian life. He has, as it happens, told us a great deal about how *Kim* came to be written. Some of the scenery came from an early journey along the road through the Himalayas towards Tibet. While he was living in America he got as far as inventing the son of an Irish soldier and calling him "Kim of the 'Rishti", which is the title of the book given on the original manuscript of it, now to be seen in the British Museum. But it is conceivable that at this time he was a little shy of attempting another. Then, after the return to England, "in a gloomy, windy autumn *Kim* came back to me with insistence, and I took it to be smoked over with my Father."

It is clearly one of the three or four of his books with which he was best satisfied — one

Rudyard Kipling

of those in the writing of which he was guided by his "Daemon" — though he gives much of the credit to Lockwood Kipling. But he did not consider it a "real novel". His parents had both told him, one with incisive wit, the other with gentle firmness, that he would be for ever incapable of it:

> Yet I dreamed for many years of building a veritable three-decker out of chosen and long-stored timber — teak, green-heart, and ten-year-old oak knees — each curve melting deliciously into the next that the sea might nowhere meet resistance or weakness; the whole suggesting motion even when, her great sails for the moment furled, she lay in some needed haven — a vessel ballasted on ingots of pure research and knowledge, roomy, filled with delicate cabinet-work below-decks, painted, carved, gilt and wreathed the length of her, from her blazing stern-galleries outlined by bronzy palm-trunks, to her rampant figure-head — an East Indiaman worthy to lie alongside . . .

Now there is obvious feeling in this unusually luxuriant passage. Kipling did wish to write such a book as he here fondly describes. It was a sorrow to him that he had never done so. But the surprise comes when he names the novel alongside which he would have liked his East Indiaman to be worthy to lie. It is *The Cloister and the Hearth*. Now I do not propose to undertake here the aim-

The Golden Years

less task of arguing whether Charles Reade's book is or is not a finer work of literature than *Kim*. But it is fair to ask in what respect it is a "real novel", while *Kim* is not. *Kim*, says its author, "of course, was nakedly picaresque and plotless — a thing imposed from without". But would not those words apply equally well to *The Cloister and the Hearth?*

The dismissal of *Kim* as not being a "real novel" seems to imply a definition of that term at which it is hard even to guess. The defects which disfigured the three attempts of the previous decade make no appearance here. The story is coherent and well proportioned and the one developing character in it, the principal character, does indeed develop in an entirely credible way. Here once and for all Kipling proved that his gift for telling stories need not have been confined to the short story. *Kim* is a long book and it is in a genre which requires particular skill and strictness in construction. The liberty which the picaresque novel seems to offer to its writer is highly deceptive. It is a fine long flexible rope with which he may, if not hang himself, at any rate tie himself into any number of knots.

Kim provides a very fine example of the picaresque controlled by an artistic intelligence with a sense of form. Of the degree of control

Rudyard Kipling

which its author exercised over it we have one revealing instance:

> There was a half-chapter of the Lama sitting down in the blue-green shadows at the foot of a glacier, telling Kim stories out of the Jatakas, which was truly beautiful, but, as my old Classics master would have said, "otiose", and it was removed almost with tears.

The gravest temptation of the writer of the picaresque story is to let "otiose" passages stand so long as they are good in themselves, whether they contribute to the movement of the tale or not. His great problem is to part the characters and to bring them together again at the proper times with a decent observance of the probabilities. The Lama's quest for the River of the Arrow and Kim's quest for the "Red Bull on a green field", followed by his enlistment in "the Great Game", provide all the machinery which is necessary for this purpose. All Kipling has to do is to convince the reader that Kim and the Lama could and would go wandering in this manner. And it is a machinery which encourages, instead of inhibiting, what is best in the picaresque form. The romance of foot-loose travel has never been expressed with more gusto, nowhere better than in the description of the end of Kim's first term at St. Xavier's. He:

The Golden Years

Yearned for the caress of soft mud squishing up between the toes, as his mouth watered for mutton stewed with butter and cabbages, for rice speckled with strong-scented cardamons, for the saffron-tinted rice, garlic and onions, and the forbidden greasy sweetmeats of the bazars.

On Lucknow station platform he watched young De Castro, all covered with prickly-heat, get into a second-class compartment. Kim patronised a third, and was the life and soul of it. He explained to the company that he was assistant to a juggler who had left him behind sick with fever, and that he would pick up his master at Umballa. As the occupants of the carriage changed, he varied this tale, or adorned it with all the shoots of a budding fancy, the more rampant for being held off native speech so long. In all India that night was no human being so joyful as Kim. At Umballa he got out and headed eastward, plashing over the sodden fields to the village where the old soldier lived.

It is in this, in the wide, thronged, coloured picture of India, in the characters of the Lama and Kim himself, and in the full gallery of the minor characters, that the attraction of the book resides. The story of Secret Service work is good enough to serve its purpose but it is instructive to observe with how firm a hand Kipling keeps it in its place. It is clearly subordinate in his mind to the other elements in the tale, and even in the final adventure

Rudyard Kipling

when Hurree Chunder Mookerjee is accompanying the spies towards Simla and Kim manages to secure their papers, it is treated with stern restraint where the writer of mere adventures would have permitted himself vastly more latitude.

If, as has been argued, it should be possible to say in a sentence what any real book is *about*, then it must be said that *Kim* is *about* the infinite and joyous variety of India for him who has eyes to see it and the heart to rejoice in it. Perhaps the key to it all is in the passage in which the old soldier conducts the Lama and Kim to the edge of the Grand Trunk Road:

"See, Holy One — the Great Road which is the backbone of all Hindustan. For the most part it is shaded, as here, with four lines of trees; the middle road — all hard — takes the quick traffic. In the days before rail-carriages the Sahibs travelled up and down here in hundreds. Now there are only country-carts and such like. Left and right is the rougher road for the heavy carts — grain and cotton and timber, bhoosa, lime and hides. A man goes in safety here — for at every few *kos* is a police-station. The police are thieves and extortioners (I myself would patrol it with cavalry — young recruits under a strong captain), but at least they do not suffer any rivals. All castes and kinds of men move here. Look! Brahmins and chumars, bankers and tinkers, barbers and bunnias,

The Golden Years

pilgrims and potters — all the world coming and going. It is to me as a river from which I am withdrawn like a log after a flood."

And truly the Grand Trunk Road is a wonderful spectacle. It runs straight, bearing without crowding India's traffic for fifteen hundred miles — such a river of life as nowhere else exists in the world. They looked at the green-arched, shade-flecked length of it, the white breadth speckled with slow-pacing folk; and the two-roomed police-station opposite.

I cannot help feeling that here we have one of the early signs of that growth of the historical sense which was so marked a characteristic of Kipling's development during these years. It is almost as though he had begun, through the eyes of the old soldier, to regard the British rule in India as an historical phenomenon as well as a present reality. This picture has a remarkable affinity to that other picture, of Hadrian's Wall, which I have already quoted. The British, to be sure, were not the original builders of the Grand Trunk Road, but it was the peace they imposed on India which allowed it to become this "river of life". Is it possible that Kipling felt the approach of a day when the Road, like the Wall, would be no more than a monument to men who had striven to do their best for the peoples over which they were called to rule?

Rudyard Kipling

But this development was itself closely connected with the general change that came over Kipling's work when he had completed the first half of his life. There was a ripening, a mellowing process in his mind, like that which occurs in the flesh of a fruit. Certain of his fundamental conceptions, as I have tried to show, were never changed. He continued to believe that it was the first, and an urgent, duty of civilisation to protect the people against war, famine and disease. He continued to believe that Parliamentary democracy, with its concomitant of rulers chosen on irrelevant grounds, would never fulfil that duty. But experience deprived him of the young man's hope that, if he set out these hopes with enough fire and force, opinion would rally to them. This deprivation did not embitter him but induced in him a new tolerance, a desire to make the best of what there is in the world and in mankind — and not only that but of all that there ever has been. This is the informing spirit of *Kim* as of all his work at this time.

Kim is, indeed, a remarkably sunny book, with a surprising dearth of dislikeable characters. The opponents of Kim and his friends in "the Great Game" are hardly to be reckoned in this category, since their appearances are so few and so brief. There is a village priest who attempts to drug and

The Golden Years

rob the Lama. There is a Church of England Army Chaplain who, in his attitude towards Kim, is curiously reminiscent of Mr. Prout. But the appearances of these are also brief. The earlier Kipling (of, for example, *Baa, Baa, Black Sheep*) could hardly have resisted introducing into Kim's schooldays at St. Xavier's some hardships and injustices, which indeed would have been probable enough. But these years, apart from the holidays, are passed over lightly enough. The author's interests are elsewhere, with Mahbub Ali, the Pathan horse-coper, with the talkative "virtuous woman" of Saharunpore, with that "fearful" Bengali, Hurree Chunder Mookerjee, with the mysterious Lurgan Sahib, and, most of all, with the Lama.

The severest test, it has been said, to which a novelist can expose himself is the portrayal of spiritual goodness. It is, to be sure, one to which wise novelists do not often expose themselves. But of those who have it would be difficult to remember many who have come through it with more success than Kipling did in his picture of the Lama. For this is goodness without anything either superhuman or insipid in it. The Lama is a man who has attained simplicity of heart in the singleness of his pursuit of the Way. He reveals himself most when he rebukes himself for a lapse of will and remembers an earlier wickedness:

"I did not seek truth in those days, but the talk of doctrine. All illusion! I drank the beer and ate the bread of Guru Ch'wan. Next day one said: 'We go out to fight Sangor Gutok down the valley to discover (mark again how Lust is tied to Anger!) which abbot shall bear rule in the valley, and take the profit of the prayers they print at Sangor Gutok.' I went, and we fought a day."

"But how, Holy One?"

"With our long pencases as I could have shown. . . . I say, we fought under the poplars, both abbots and all the monks, and one laid open my forehead to the bone. See!" He tilted back his cap and showed a puckered silvery scar. "Just and perfect is the Wheel! Yesterday the scar itched, and after fifty years I recalled how it was dealt and the face of him who dealt it; dwelling a little in illusion. Followed that which thou didst see — strife and stupidity. Just is the Wheel! The idolater's blow fell upon the scar. Then I was shaken in my soul: my soul was darkened, and the boat of my soul rocked upon the waters of illusion. Not till I came to Shamlegh could I meditate upon the Cause of Things, or trace the running grass-roots of Evil. I strove all the long night."

"But, Holy One, thou art innocent of all evil. May I be thy sacrifice!"

The Golden Years

By the Lama and by the love which he and Kim feel for one another, the love expressed in this last exclamation, the book must ultimately stand or fall. And this makes it necessary that Kim should be something more than the mere subject of the verb "to wander" which the hero of the picaresque novel often is. He is, in fact, a credible, well-modelled, living character. He is, of course, exceptional in innate qualities as well as in his upbringing, but Kipling writes convincingly of his qualities. What is important is that the reader does see him grow, during the three years or so which the book covers, until he is ready to support the trial which is its climax.

III

It is noticeable that Kipling associated with *Kim* and the two *Jungle Books,* as having been written under the special care of his "Daemon" *Puck of Pook's Hill* and *Rewards and Fairies* — "Good care I took to walk delicately lest he should withdraw. I know that he did not, because when those books were finished they said so themselves with, almost, the water-hammer click of a tap turned off." It is noticeable, too, that he speaks of the how and why of these stories with a confiding amplitude he shows nowhere else, even *Kim* taking a second place:

> Since the tales had to be read by children, before people realised that they were meant for grown-ups; and since they had to be a sort of balance to, as well as a seal upon, some aspects of my "Imperialistic" output in the past, I worked the material in three or four overlaid tints and textures, which might or might not reveal themselves according to the shifting light of sex, youth and experience. It was like working lacquer and mother o' pearl, a natural combination, into the same scheme as niello and grisaille, and trying not to let the joins show.
>
> So I loaded the book up with allegories and allusions, and verified references until my old Chief would have been almost pleased with me; put in three or four really good sets of verses. . . .

The last clause is endearing enough to make one chuckle with pleasure. Kipling now brought his practice of wedding prose and verse to its height. The poems contained in these two books include many of the best he ever wrote. Removed from the books they make an admirable sequence. But they are happiest and most effective sitting side by side with the stories to which they belong. These twenty-one stories and thirty-eight poems make a single work. To this statement there should be one reservation. Kipling says that *If*

The Golden Years

"escaped from the book and for a while ran about the world". It is, with its epigrammatic efficiency, a good poem and, like a good poem, it knew when it was out of place.

This single work, which, for simplicity's sake, I propose to call simply *Puck*, is Kipling's final picture of the England he had come to love and which had in a measure, if perhaps on a different plane, taken for him the place of the Empire he had previously worshipped. That Empire had shown itself a rather uncertain object for his affections. Here was something solid with its roots deep in time. Because he loved it so much he wanted to understand its growth and that he could do only by describing it. When England stood to her defences in 1914, he wrote of "the ages' slow-bought gain". *Puck* is in effect an explanation of what he meant.

It had, as he says, to be read first by children. Above all, it had to be read. The certainty of this inspired him to give it as happy an opening as can be conceived. Dan and Una, who live in Sussex, have the luck to perform the one spell which will bring Puck to them and make him say: "What on Human Earth made you act in *Midsummer Night's Dream* three times over, *on* Midsummer Eve, *in* the middle of a Ring, and under — right *under* one of my oldest hills in old

Rudyard Kipling

England?" Having been thus summoned, he gives the children seizin:

"Now are you two lawfully seized and possessed of all Old England," began Puck, in a sing-song voice. "By right of Oak, Ash, and Thorn are you free to come and go and look and know where I shall show or best you please. You shall see What you shall see and you shall hear What you shall hear, though It shall have happened three thousand year; and you shall know neither Doubt nor Fear. Fast! Hold fast all I give you."

Then he shows them scene after scene out of the history of their country — though, with great tact, not in chronological order, which might have made even the grown-ups for whom the book was eventually intended regard it askance as a series of history-lessons.

It was a fairly formidable task which Kipling had undertaken, one which the poetic gift could not compass by itself. Lockwood Kipling, while they were thinking it over in silence, said suddenly, "And you'll have to look up your references rather more carefully, won't you?" Kipling must have done so. He used sometimes what he called "ligitimate inferences" as when he asserted that the Seventh Cohort of the Thirtieth (Ulpia Victrix) Legion was quartered on the Wall, an inference

The Golden Years

afterwards substantiated by an inscription. So far as I know, there has been no criticism of his facts, though his interpretation of them is naturally open to question by those who take different views.[1]

Quite early the main themes are announced. One is the theme of age and continuity:

"It must have been some few years later — a year or two before the Conquest, I think — that I came to Pook's Hill here, and one evening I heard old Hobden talking about Weland's Ford."

"If you mean old Hobden the hedger, he's only seventy-two. He told me so himself," said Dan. "He's an intimate friend of ours."

"You're quite right," Puck replied. "I meant old Hobden's ninth great-grandfather. He was a free man and burned charcoal hereabouts. I've known the family, father and son, so long that I get confused sometimes. Hob of the Dene was my Hobden's name, and he lived at the Forge cottage.

The other is the theme of loyalty and service. Hugh in *The Tree of Justice*, even in the presence of the grim King Henry, is not afraid to show his

---

[1] I have, however, myself caught him in a minor slip. Parnesius says: "Our Villa's on the South edge of the Island by the Broken Cliffs. Most of it is three hundred years old, but the cow-stables, where our first ancestor lived, must be a hundred years older. Oh, quite that, because the founder of our family had his land given him by Agricola at the Settlement." Parnesius says this during the reign of Gratian as Emperor in the West and makes his Villa about a hundred years older than it could have been.

Rudyard Kipling

loyalty to Harold the Saxon who is discovered as an old and crazed wanderer and dies on Hugh's breast. Hal o' the Draft, though he diverges from the true path for a moment, is loyal to his work and finds that loyalty so much enough for him that he only laughs when he discovers that the King has knighted him because of the carefulness that has saved thirty pounds and not because he is a master craftsman. The young men on the Wall hold to their trust though there is treachery behind them and ruin in front. The downland man of the Flint Age gives his eye for an iron knife which his people may use to defend themselves from the wolves and, worse than that, has to submit to being regarded by them as a god and beyond all human kindnesses and pleasures.

Perhaps the most striking example of what Kipling has to say in these stories is to be found in *Young Men at the Manor*. Sir Richard Dalyngridge, who came over with the Conqueror, goes skirmishing on after the battle at Santlache[1] and finds himself alone. He fights with a Saxon and spares his life. Next the Saxon saves Richard's life from a fierce wandering group of his own countrymen and takes him home to the Manor.

[1] I hope Kipling did verify his references here, for the practice of calling the Battle of Hastings Senlac has been much blown upon lately.

The Golden Years

Here it is found that Hugh the Saxon is sorely wounded. His sister, the Lady Aelueva, declares that if he dies Richard shall hang. Her men set upon Richard and he is bound and spends the night with a halter round his neck. In the morning he is rescued by Gilbert de Aquila to whom he makes excuses for his captors — on account of the Lady Aelueva. De Aquila laughs and says:

"Look, men — a miracle. The fight is scarce sped, my father is not yet buried, and here we find our youngest knight already set down in his Manor, while his Saxons — ye can see it in their fat faces — have paid him homage and service! By the Saints," he said, rubbing his nose, "I never thought England would be so easy won! Surely I can do no less than give the lad what he has taken. This Manor shall be thine, boy," he said, "till I come again, or till thou art slain."

He rides away, leaving Richard to hold his new possession with the help of his thirty men-at-arms. Here we have the subaltern sent off with a small detachment, responsible alone both for the safety of his men and for the execution of his orders. Then his men want to hang the three Saxons who put the halter round his neck. It is a difficult moment, but:

As I stood doubting a woman ran down from the oak wood above the King's Hill yonder, and cried out

Rudyard Kipling

that some Normans were driving off the swine there.

"Norman or Saxon," said I, "we must beat them back, or they will rob us every day. Out at them with any arms ye have!" So I loosed those three carles and we ran together, my men-at-arms and the Saxons with bills and bows which they had hidden in the thatch of their huts, and Hugh led them. Halfway up the King's Hill we found a false fellow from Picardy — a sutler that sold wine in the Duke's camp — with a dead knight's shield on his arm, a stolen horse under him, and some ten or twelve wastrels at his tail, all cutting and slashing at the pigs. We beat them off, and saved our pork. One hundred and seventy pigs we saved in that great battle.

After the "great battle" Hugh says to Richard: "Thou hast gone far to conquer England this evening", and Richard answers: "England must be thine and mine, then. Help me, Hugh, to deal aright with these people." England, as we have her today, is the result of a long process of growth, in which the man of the Flint Age and Parnesius and Hugh and Richard all had their early parts. These things, Kipling says, spring from the soil and pass into it again and enrich it.

It may seem that I have somewhat overemphasised the didactic element in these stories. The method of summary and comment does, it must be confessed, inevitably mean the chemical isolation

The Golden Years

of the powder from the jam. But after all the powder is there, and Kipling put it there, well knowing what he was doing. He owns as much when he tells us that he had to contrive that *Puck* should be read by children first so that it might be read by grown-ups later. In fact, his whole habit of mind, all his life, was didactic. The element of teaching is assuredly not more obtrusive here than it was in the stories in which he exemplified his Imperialism in its earlier phase. The whole work is undoubtedly meant to convey a lesson. In reading it one is reminded strongly of some words written by one of Kipling's contemporaries, one between whom and Kipling himself it is at several points tempting to make comparisons. "Those who read me", said Conrad, "know my conviction that the world, the temporal world, rests on a few very simple ideas; so simple that they must be as old as the hills. It rests notably, among others, on the idea of fidelity." Kipling was not much given to explaining so explicitly as this what were his intentions in what he wrote, but if he had been he might have said something very much like this. In that sense, and in the fullness of that sense, he was always a didactic writer, a preacher, a moralist. Like all artists, he worked continuously at the establishment of an attitude towards life

Rudyard Kipling

and in the artist an attitude towards life is indistinguishable from a morality.

He preached love of England because he found that it fostered the growth of the virtues he regarded as necessary for the world. He was not a merely sentimental patriot: he was an uncompromising and sometimes disconcerting realist where his own country was concerned. He proclaimed that when he wrote the lines quoted above about England being what England seems. *Puck* is really his answer to the charge that England is "only putty, brass and paint". She is not, she is the creation of the men and women who are presented in these stories.

It is true that, for his picture, Kipling takes the best. He tells us how Sir Richard Dalyngridge protected the manorial pigs but nothing of how in later days Sir Richard's descendants may have oppressed and exploited the manorial serfs. But then in essence this book is a love-poem. The lover who says that his mistress is "holy, wise and fair" is surely not required to assert also that there are other women who are none of these things — or even that she herself has her bad moods. The activities of Kipling's good men and women in *Puck* postulate the plentiful existence of others who were not so good — as, for example, the sutler on his stolen horse. Kipling celebrates here those

The Golden Years

who have helped to make England what she is. He presents examples.

The book is, I repeat, a love-poem — and it is not a statement on the course of English history sworn before a Commissioner of Oaths. It has the congruous decorations which a lover adds to the direct expression of his passion. Many of these are easily isolated from the stories themselves. The landscapes here are among the best he ever painted. Each piece has a little introduction, in the course of which the children are thrown back into the past, and if these could be detached from their context, they would make by themselves a delicious gallery of country scenes. For a specimen I take that in which the children hang on behind Cattiwow's timber-tug as it goes into the woods:

The wood road beyond the brook climbs at once into the woods, and you see all the horses' backs rising, one above another, like moving stairs. Cattiwow strode ahead in his sackcloth woodman's petticoat, belted at the waist with a leather strap; and when he turned and grinned, his red lips showed under his sackcloth-coloured beard. His cap was sackcloth too, with a flap behind, to keep twigs and bark out of his neck. He navigated the tug among pools of heather-water that splashed in their faces, and through clumps of young birches that slashed at their legs, and when they hit an old toadstooled stump, they never knew whether

Rudyard Kipling

it would give way in showers of rotten wood, or jar them back again.

But, if we are to pursue the analogy, the poems inserted in the work provide its lilt, the final enchantment. With the addition of a few pieces from elsewhere, *The Recall* being the most notable of them, they contain the essence of what Kipling had to say about England — an England which stretches through time as well as across space. Perhaps he was only just in time to write them. It can hardly be a mere coincidence that two of his contemporaries, Robert Bridges and A. E. Housman, have, in their own ways, but with the same elusively nostalgic note, made comparable records of the English countryside which was being mightily changed as they wrote.

Kipling's touch was not sure at the beginning. The famous, too famous, poem *Sussex* uses a little too much brass in its orchestra. The first four lines provide good doctrine and a text on which Kipling was to write a good many sermons:

> God gave all men all earth to love,
>   But since our hearts are small,
> Ordained for each one spot should prove
>   Beloved over all.

But the second verse runs from the Baltic to "Levuka's Trade", and in the third "our blunt,

The Golden Years

bow-headed, whale-backed Downs", vivid as it is, conjures up a wholly incongruous image.

That was written before Kipling quite realised that he had come home from the world to settle in England. (It is to be noted that the arrangement of his collected poems keeps it far apart from the poems in *Puck*.) He soon found that a softer music was needed, the music of *The Way Through the Woods:*

> They shut the road through the woods
> Seventy years ago.
> Weather and rain have undone it again,
> And now you would never know
> There was once a road through the woods
> Before they planted the trees.
> It is underneath the coppice and heath,
> And the thin anemones.
> Only the keeper sees
> That, where the ring-dove broods,
> And the badgers roll at ease,
> There was once a road through the woods.
>
> Yet, if you enter the woods
> Of a summer evening late,
> When the night-air cools on the trout-ringed pools
> Where the otter whistles his mate,
> (They fear not men in the woods,
> Because they see so few.)
> You will hear the beat of a horse's feet,

Rudyard Kipling

And the swish of a skirt in the dew,
Steadily cantering through
The misty solitudes,
As though they perfectly knew
The old lost road through the woods . . .
But there is no road through the woods.

This is a melody which cannot be played, to use the phrase of the 'Nineties, on a banjo. It is the melody, however, which was most natural to Kipling when he was at the height of his powers and moved by the theme which he felt most deeply. I have spoken of a "nostalgic note" and have suggested that he was only just in time to write these poems. But in the mood in which he wrote them he would very likely not have flinched from admitting that they were in the nature of a farewell music. (*Sussex*, written before them in 1902, praises the Downs as being "clean of officious fence or hedge" — saying nothing of bungalows or the wire that saves a shepherd's wages!) But he thought of this music as a farewell to something which goes to come again. He had faithfully made his own record of the things which seemed to him to be ineradicable from English soil. His own time thought of him chiefly as a prophet of modernity. But a future generation may prefer to think of him as a remembrance of what survives modernity. If it does it will turn

The Golden Years

first for proof to the poem which Kipling in the collected poems quite erroneously describes as having been the Prelude to *Puck of Pook's Hill:*

> Cities and Thrones and Powers
>   Stand in Time's eye,
> Almost as long as flowers,
>   Which daily die:
> But, as new buds put forth
>   To glad new men,
> Out of the spent and unconsidered Earth,
>   The Cities rise again.

This, in its combination of resignation and hope, is a perfect expression of the sense of history which Kipling had now acquired.

CHAPTER VII

Sunset and After-Glow

In 1913 KIPLING published a story called *The Edge of the Evening*. It is not one of his best but there is a reason for mentioning it in a survey from which so many better pieces have to be omitted. It describes how a German aeroplane, after taking illicit photographs, came down in the park of a country-house in the south of England, and how its occupants, foolish enough to shoot at the members of the house-party who found them, were accidentally killed — one of them by a blow from a golf-club, the other in a Rugger tackle. Their bodies were replaced in the aeroplane and an American, who happened to be present and who happened also to have designed the engine, managed to get them into the air again with the hope that they would fall into the Channel. One character in the story says:

Sunset and After-Glow

It'll make an infernal international stink. What did I tell you in the smoking-room after lunch? The tension's at breaking-point already. This 'ud snap it.

Thus, a year before the Great War broke out, Kipling was ready for it and the warning which this story conveys is, in retrospect, all the more impressive for its twilight setting. He had indeed dreaded it for a long time. He knew that it would be horribly unlike the wars of which he had dreamt in earlier days — the wars in which Stalky, with a handful of Sikhs, was to work miracles. How much he had dreaded it is revealed in his immediate reaction to it:

> No easy hope or lies
> Shall bring us to our goal,
> But iron sacrifice
> Of body, will, and soul.
> There is but one task for all —
> One life for each to give.
> What stands if Freedom fall?
> Who dies if England live?

In this position he stood and fought it out by such means as were possible for him. But there is another line in the same poem: "Our world has passed away", which has its own deep meaning. Kipling had made for himself images of two worlds.

Rudyard Kipling

In the first the White Man carried his Burden towards the millennium. In the second, England blossomed and regenerated the world by her example. And now he was faced, as he had feared that he would be, by "steel and fire and stone".

Now, as not in the South African War, he wrote in the polemic spirit, even savagely. When it was falsely reported that the German Emperor was dying, like his father, of cancer in the throat, he wrote without mercy:

"This is the State above the Law.
    The State exists for the State alone."
  (*This is a gland at the back of the jaw,*
    And an answering lump by the collar-bone.)

Some die shouting in gas or fire;
  Some die silent, by shell or shot.
Some die desperate, caught on the wire;
  Some die suddenly. This will not.

"Regis suprema voluntas Lex."
    (*It will follow the natural course of — throats.*)
  Some die pinned by the broken decks,
    Some die sobbing between the boats.

There was in Kipling a cruelty towards the enemy during the Great War which he had never shown before. Mary Postgate, a gentle-natured woman, carries on steadily with her work in hand,

Sunset and After-Glow

knowing that a crashed German airman is dying slowly a little distance from her. Maddingham in *Sea Constables* relentlessly chivvies a "neutral" vessel, carrying oil for German submarines, up and down the Irish Channel until her owner falls desperately ill and puts into a small Irish port. There he begs for mercy, to be taken to where he can get medical help:

"I said: 'Look here! I'm a middle-aged man, and I don't suppose my conscience is any clearer than yours in many respects, but this is business. I can do nothing for you.' "

"You got that a bit mixed, I think," said Tegg critically.

"*He* saw what I was driving at," Maddingham replied, "and he was the only one that mattered for the moment. 'Then I'm a dead man, Mr. Maddingham,' he said. 'That's *your* business,' I said. 'Good afternoon.' And I went out."

"And?" said Winchmore, after some silence.

"He died. I saw his flag half-masted next morning."

In these tales there is a grim relish indicative of strong passion.

It was the destruction of good, useful and innocent lives which above all tormented him — even before he had lost his only son. It is fitting

Rudyard Kipling

that the best of his war-work should be found in a series of exquisite epitaphs, such as:

THE BEGINNER
> On the first hour of my first day
> In the front trench I fell.
> (Children in boxes at a play
>   Stand up to watch it well.)

and:

V.A.D. (MEDITERRANEAN)
> Ah, would swift ships had never been, for then we ne'er had found,
> These harsh Aegean rocks between, this little virgin drowned,
> Whom neither spouse nor child shall mourn, but men she nursed through pain
> And — certain keels for whose return the heathen look in vain.

Even here the note of angry vengeance is sounded.

There were, to be sure, consolations for Kipling even in these times. In one thing he had made no miscalculation. It was true as ever it had been that the English were sound and stubborn stuff and quite ready to fight for what they valued. He went the round of the New Armies in training and he, who knew so much of the life of the Old Army, was rejoiced by the novelties he saw:

Sunset and After-Glow

"Mm!" said the military policeman. "The more a man has in his head, the harder it is for him to manage his carcass — at first. I'm glad I never was a sergeant. Listen to the instructors! Like rooks, ain't it?"

There was a mile of sergeants and instructors, varied by company officers, all at work on the ready material under their hands. They grunted, barked, yapped, expostulated, and, in rare cases, purred, as the lines broke and formed and wheeled over the vast maidan. When companies numbered off one could hear the tone and accent of every walk in life, and maybe half the counties of England, from the deep-throated "Woon" of the North to the sharp, half-whistled Devonshire "Tu." And as the instructors laboured, so did the men, with a passion to learn as passionately as they were taught.

But it infuriated him that this fine material should be put to the wasteful purposes of what he already regarded as an anachronism. He felt a passion of hatred against the people who had involved the world in this misery and loss.

II

As had happened to him before, the experience of the War helped to ripen in him changes that had already begun. And now we reach Kipling's final, most difficult, least understood period, in which, as usual, it will be necessary to include things that were written before the War. It hardly needs to be added that frequently among the post-War pieces we find recapitulations, returns to earlier themes and moods, such as are to be expected in the last work of an old man.

We are all rather mealy-mouthed nowadays about the application of the word "old" to individuals, just as we are hopefully vague about the use of the word "middle-aged". Absurd as it may seem, I cannot help feeling that the phrase "the last work of an old man" suits ill with the fact that Kipling was only seventy when he died and that much of the work of which I am speaking was done when he was in his fifties and sixties and some of it even earlier. But there is one thing that makes it easier for us to see why in his last period he showed many of the characteristics which, when fortune is kind, distinguish the artist who has grown not merely old but very old in the practice of his art. His precocity followed him to the end. He had full fifty years as a practising artist of high achievement. Problems of technique yielded to him very early. In the first of his middle years he found himself able to deal very handsomely and fruitfully with problems of temperament and character. He advanced rapidly to that stage in the growth of the mind which is

Sunset and After-Glow

what we mean when we talk about the very old artist — a stage in which all that is posssible has been done and the impossible beckons with an enticing finger.

What this stage of growth means to the individual who has experienced it is, probably, something that can never be told by anyone else. And those who have experienced never do tell, except in riddles obscurely and impatiently phrased. They feel that they have other things to do with their time. When this point in an author's development begins, the critic has a curious sensation as though his subject were escaping from him into a mist. Hitherto the author has walked at the reader's side, at a reasonable pace, discoursing in intelligible language about the countryside through which they are passing. But now they approach together a region of drifting cloud and the author seems to be possessed by a strange, almost an irrational, eagerness. He hurries ahead, too fast for his companion, shouting sometimes over his shoulder phrases that are not easily understood and that seem not to have been put together as well as they might have been. The critic must follow as best he can, increasingly uncertain of his footing and oppressed by the thought that one who was a wise and enchanting guide seems to have taken leave of both senses and manners. And yet sometimes the author stands and utters a sentence of simple sound and of simple import, almost as though he wanted to prove that he is still sane, even if not always in a manner that his companion can understand. But even these utterances often have disturbing overtones. One such is Kipling's *Something of Myself*, of which I shall have little to say in this chapter because there is so little in it that is characteristic of the last period. But it contains one sentence, and that the last, which (I can put it in no other way) knocks the reader backwards. For several pages Kipling has been describing in an agreeable and gossiping manner the tools of his trade, pens and pen-wipers and the like, and the room in which he kept them. Then he says:

> Left and right of the table were two big globes, on one of which a great airman had once outlined in white paint those air-routes to the East and Australia which were well in use before my death.

The shape of the chapter, and indeed of the whole book, would seem to suggest that only by accident was the writing interrupted here, that there was an intention to continue it at some future opportunity which never occurred. It is assuredly, from any ordinary standpoint, a startlingly abrupt conclusion to a book which throughout displays

Sunset and After-Glow

its author as being in a peaceful, even a serene, state of mind. I am tempted to conjecture that Kipling set out to end his sentence with the equivalent of some such commonplace phrase as "even during my own life-time". But his "Daemon" intervened to suggest the other phrase and when he had written it he could not allow any orderly rounding out of the book to destroy its enormous and mysterious effect. The old artist behaves in this manner because he is more interested in what he can see than in communicating it to anyone else. He does, of course, take some interest in communicating it or he would not write at all. But the mere effort of seeing all the things that are being revealed to him takes up so much of his time and energy, that he finds it hard to write more than baffling scribbles. It frequently happens, too, that, afraid of being misunderstood, he deliberately makes himself hard to understand.

It is, however, possible to say what were the themes which most interested Kipling at the end of his life. He was concerned with the immortal problems of pain and death, of ill-doing and punishment, of the other world, and of religion. No doubt the War must in any case have quickened the sensitiveness of every mind towards these problems. But there is no mistaking the fact that Kipling chose a particular approach to them, an

Rudyard Kipling

approach to which he would eventually have come even if there had never been any War. This particular approach takes the form of a preoccupation with the accidents to which the human machine is liable — both in the flesh and in the mind.

One of the stories in his last collection appears to be on the surface, as indeed he incidentally proclaims it to be, his sole attempt at the detective-story. A girl is found killed beside a country road, with a hole neatly punched in the back of her head, and two men set out in search of the murderer. Her death is at last found to be due to a queer but quite convincing accident. In earlier days Kipling would have been quite content with such a story to tell. If we consider it purely as a competently told story, it would probably have been safer in his hands then. But here the emphasis is laid on a man who is wrongly suspected of being the criminal, and it is so laid because Kipling is interested in a complicated mental condition resulting from shell-shock.

This is, to be sure, a fault in artistry. Each part of the story is beautifully done, but each wastefully distracts interest from the other. Can one, however, say that this is a fault in the artist? No — because there are now matters which concern him more than perfection in story-telling.

Sunset and After-Glow

His simple mechanical problem in detection has led him to the problem of the bedevilment of a human mind. Impatiently engrossed by this he cares little what effect is produced on the reader. He is the old artist, hurrying on through the mists. Let his companion follow as best he can. And even if the companion does find it a rather difficult task, that will perhaps the more impress on him the truth that life's ultimate puzzles are difficult indeed.

In this story, at the end, Kipling shows full mercy to the victim. In *Dayspring Mishandled* he does nothing of the sort: he shows no mercy to anyone concerned, not even to the narrator. Of all the compositions of his final years, there is none providing a better example of his deliberate subtlety and obscurity.

As well as I can understand it, the tale is this. There was a woman associated with, and much loved by, a certain literary "Bohemian" set. One member of the set, Manallace, who loved her more than the others, made himself responsible for her when she lost her health. Another, Castorley, who had risen since then, replied to an appeal for help that he had "known the lady very slightly and the calls on his purse were so heavy, that, etc." Later this second man said something, unquoted, to the first, which we must understand as having been

Rudyard Kipling

insulting to the lady. The first then conceived a campaign of vengeance which engaged him for years and cost him infinite pains. This campaign involved him in the necessity of writing verses which could pass for Chaucer's — of which Kipling gives us a specimen:

> To-bruized be that slender, sterting spray
> Out of the oake's rind that should betide
> A branch of girt and goodliness, straightway
> Her spring is turned on herself, and wried
> And knotted like some gall or veiney wen. —
> Dayspring mishandled cometh not agen.

It involved a careful study of the methods of the copyists of Chaucer, as expounded by the intended victim. Then the avenger had to compound an ink such as was used at that time, and a paste with traces of stone-grit in it. Having done all this he must plant the forgery where it would come to the notice of the victim. The combination of the theme of revenge with an absorption in technicalities is peculiarly characteristic of Kipling at all times.

But at this point the story takes an unexpected turn. The pitfall has been dug and the victim has fallen into it. The fragment has been entrusted to his care and he explains: "Was there ever anything in literary finds to hold a candle

Sunset and After-Glow

to it? And they give grocers knighthoods for selling cheese!" It is "public recognition" that he wants and Manallace, still indefatigable, helps him to get it. Castorley becomes Sir Alured and imperatively enlists Manallace as his principal assistant. The first uneasiness comes into Manallace's mind when he begins to suspect that Lady Castorley knows the truth. The uneasiness grows when she presses for the early publication of what she must know, if his suspicion is correct, to be something which will blast her husband's reputation. And, since Castorley's health is failing, in the disturbingly sinister manner which Kipling at this time so well knew how to convey, it may do more than that. It may quite possibly kill him out of hand. Gradually it comes to Manallace that Lady Castorley hates her husband and would like to see him dead, and, by a final touch of horror, that it is the surgeon who is attending Castorley who is Lady Castorley's lover. The nightmare is ended by Castorley's death of "malignant kidney-trouble, generalised at the end". Manallace has arranged for the book to be published under his supervision, with all the credit to Castorley and all the profits to his widow.

I am far from being sure that, out of Kipling's quart-pot, I have poured into my gill-measure even so much as is necessary for the purposes of my argument. I have tried to convey the feeling that it is, in the bare bones of it, a horrible story. But there is more horror than is contained in the bare bones. A horror different from that of facts pervades the whole story. Castorley's dissolution, for all that it is, described in only a few pitilessly casual details, is dwelt upon not as part of the mechanics of the plot but as though it were something important and even fascinating in itself. And Manallace makes the blood run cold when he says off-handedly: "Oh — my position? I've been dead since — April, Fourteen, it was."

Judging by ordinary technical canons, we might easily dismiss *Dayspring Mishandled* as a bad piece of story-telling. And we might as easily condemn it as a story about morbid people conceived by a mind with more than a streak of morbidity in it. But to do either of these things would be to miss the point. The story is effective to this degree that the reader, having begun it, must go through it to the end and, having finished it, cannot help remembering it, just as he remembers the most sinister incidents in a nightmare. This is because, whatever demerits it may have, it is full of the sincerity of the old questioning artist. Kipling appears throughout to be asking: But what does it all mean? And perhaps he thinks he has caught a glimpse of an answer, of which, however, he can

Sunset and After-Glow

give us no more than a bafflingly cloudier glimpse. It is no valid condemnation of him to say that he writes of people in morbid states of body and mind. For most people the whole interesting business of life ends in a morbid state of body or mind and sometimes of both. Kipling asked: Why? What does it all mean?

There is no need here to labour by repeated examples the fascination exercised on him by malignant disease. In an earlier story he had written: "Human nature seldom walks up to the word 'cancer'". Now he did walk up to it again and again. "Auntie Armine", in *A Madonna of the Trenches*, sends by her nephew a message to her secret lover at the front, who is the boy's sergeant:

" 'Well, then, tell 'im from me,' she says, 'that I expect to be through with my little trouble by the twenty-first of next month, an' I'm dyin' to see him as soon as possible after that date.' "

"What sort of trouble was it?" Keede turned professional at once.

"She'd 'ad a bit of a gatherin' in 'er breast, I believe. But she never talked of 'er body much to anyone."

The sergeant is due to go on leave on the twenty-first. He begins his journey but does not go far. He is found poisoned by charcoal-fumes in a dug-out. But before that he repeats mysteriously to the boy, "If after the manner of men, I have fought with beasts at Ephesus, what advantageth it me, if the dead rise not?" And this text might almost be the motto for the work of Kipling's last years. He had seen a glorious pageant of life, men and women and countries. But what — the question dwelt with him — was it all for?

III

Like all writers of the short-story he had dealt in the supernatural from his earliest years. *The Phantom Rickshaw* was one of his first tales. *At the End of the Passage* and *The Mark of the Beast* came not much later. But these were, in the sense in which that word was used about Kipling then, only "anecdotes". They showed considerable powers of invention and the technical ability to produce a shudder. But they offered no evidence of any spiritual disturbance in the mind of the writer and they left none in that of the reader. They were "thrillers", meant for entertainment only, postulating, as is necessary, when the supernatural is used for purposes of entertainment, "the willing suspension of disbelief".

Perhaps *The Brushwood Boy* should be classified with these. Yet it is written to a richer and

Sunset and After-Glow

subtler music. It is the story of a young man and a young woman who, but for a casual encounter as children which neither of them remembers, have no knowledge of one another, yet have for years shared the same dreams. Fate brings them together. Recognition is established. There is neither explanation nor any hint of a search for one. Probably this piece should be considered chiefly important as one of Kipling's earliest handlings of English life and landscape as a background. But, looking back, we can hardly help thinking of it also as having been written by the man who was going to write *They*.

They is a beautifully wrought story. Its maker loved it so much that he lavished on it all the decoration it could carry. Thus:

There came at last a brilliant day, swept clear from the south-west, that brought the hills within hand's reach — a day of unstable airs and high filmy clouds. Through no merit of my own I was free, and set the car for the third time on that known road. As I reached the crest of the Downs I felt the soft air change, saw it glaze under the sun; and, looking down at the sea, in that instant beheld the blue of the Channel turn through polished silver and dulled steel to dingy pewter. A laden collier hugging the coast steered outward for deeper water, and, across copper-coloured haze, I saw sails rise one by one on the anchored fishing-fleet. In a deep dene behind me an eddy of sudden wind drummed through sheltered oaks, and spun aloft the first dry sample of autumn leaves. When I reached the beach road the sea-fog fumed over the brickfields, and the tide was telling all the grasses of the gale beyond Ushant. In less than an hour summer England vanished in chill grey. We were again the shut island of the North, all the ships of the world bellowing at our perilous gates; and between their outcries ran the piping of bewildered gulls.

Let us here remember what Kipling said about the *Puck* stories: "I worked the material in three or four overlaid tints and textures, which might or might not reveal themselves according to the shifting light of sex, youth and experience". There are, clearly, at least three elements in *They*, if not more. One of these is its lovely decoration. Another is the story of a woman blind since a few months after birth, who lived in a beautiful house and kept it for the ghosts of children untimely dead. This was a story certain to draw tears from all sorts of eyes. But there is much more than that beyond. The only question is: What is it?

There is undoubtedly an element of the sinister. A child is ill and the narrator uses his car to fetch a doctor, then waits for the result:

Sunset and After-Glow

A woman, wiping the suds off her arms, came out of the cottage next the sweetmeat shop.

"I've be'n listenin' in de back-yard," she said cheerily. "He says Arthur's unaccountable bad. Did ye hear him shruck just now? Unaccountable bad. I reckon 'twill come Jenny's turn to walk in de wood nex' week along, Mr. Madden."

"Excuse me, Sir, but your lap-robe is slipping," said Madden deferentially. The woman started, dropped a curtsey, and hurried away.

"What does she mean by 'walking in the wood'?" I asked.

"It must be some saying they use hereabouts," said Madden. "They're an independent lot in this county. She took you for a chauffeur, Sir."

Jenny is the (unmarried) mother of the child that is believed to be dying. The wood is that which belongs to the blind woman who keeps open house for children whom neither she nor anyone else can see.

In a final scene the blind woman brings matters to a head by crying, "Oh, you *must* bear or lose. There is no other way — and yet they love me. They must! Don't they?" And then:

"You think it was wrong, then?" she cried sharply, though I had said nothing.

"Not for you. A thousand times no. For you it is

right. . . . I am grateful to you beyond words. For me it would be wrong. For me only. . . ."

"Why?" she said, but passed her hand before her face as she had done at our second meeting in the wood. "Oh, I see," she went on simply as a child. "For you it would be wrong." Then with a little indrawn laugh, "and d'you remember, I called you lucky — once — at first. You who must never come here again!"

At the end this story reveals itself as the expression, all the more poignant because of its elaborate reticence, of a personal grief. That is only one aspect of it, however. If we look at it from another point of view, we can see how the author has preserved himself from growing too egotistic by working "the material in three or four overlaid tints and textures, which might or might not reveal themselves according to the shifting light of sex, youth and experience." Looking at it from yet another point, we can see how early Kipling began to be preoccupied with those problems of pain, death and loss — problems which led direct to the main theme of his last years.

And the main theme of his last years is the possibility of there being a consolation somewhere for the evils of pain, death and loss. He explored in various directions. His explorations into the region of the supernatural may be regarded chiefly

Sunset and After-Glow

as symbolism. On an even more symbolistic plane he made up a mythology of his own, a Heaven of his own, a Universe in which justice was dealt out in accordance with the fundamental ideas from which he never in the whole of his life departed. *On the Gate*, written in 1916, shows the Angel of Death and St. Peter discussing the new responsibilities which have been thrust on their departments by the War. Death shows St. Peter his expanded staff and St. Peter takes Death to see how the new arrivals are handled at the Gate. In *Uncovenanted Mercies* Satan exhibits with pride to Azrael and Gabriel one of his ingenious contrivances — a replica of a railway terminus:

A large number of persons in Time have weaknesses for making engagements — on oath, I regret to say — to meet other persons for all Eternity. Most of these appointments are forgotten or overlaid by later activities which have first claim on our attention. But the residue — say two per cent — comes here. Naturally, it represents a high level of character, passion and tenacity which, *ipso facto*, reacts generously to our treatments. At first we used to put 'em in pillories and chaff 'em. When coaches came in, we accommodated them in replicas of roadside inns. With the advance of transportation, we duplicated all the leading London stations. (You ought to see some of 'em on a Saturday night!) But that's

Rudyard Kipling

a detail. The essence of our idea is that every soul here is waiting for a train, which may or may not bring the person with whom they have contracted to spend Eternity. And, as the English say, they don't half have to wait either.

In these stories we have set another remarkable example of Kipling's trick of painting his pictures with one tint laid over another. An idea of conduct and reward of suffering and redemption is projected by means of a mocking machinery, with yet an insistent note of pity in the sound of the machine.

This light-hearted mythology shows but one side of the Kipling of the later years. There is another in the stories which definitely show him as a man who sought for a Church. He was always a man to whom co-operation was the essence of religion or, perhaps better, the soil out of which religion springs. The sense of brotherhood was strong in him when he founded the alliance which united Beetle, Stalky and Turkey. It needs little imagination to see that, whatever else may be said, the alliance was a real thing and that Beetle found the cement for it. Without him the other two would have drifted into, and out of, all manner of other friendships, as schoolboys commonly do. Throughout his life he displayed a particular sensitiveness for any sort of

Sunset and After-Glow

freemasonry. His feeling can be summarised in Mowgli's call: "We be of one blood, thou and I!" It is significant that Mowgli had been taught to utter this call to all manner of created beings. During most of his life, Kipling showed a desire to be accepted by almost every freemasonry that he encountered. Towards the end of it he sought quite plainly for one in which he could find fulfilment and peace, the answer to the questions which old age put inexorably before him. A glimpse of this seeking occurs in the stories in which we are introduced into "the Lodge of Instruction (attached to Faith and Works E.C. 5837*)", where soldiers on leave from the front are received as Visiting Brothers. The narrator is asked to help in the work of proving these applicants:

My last man nearly broke me down altogether. Everything seemed to have gone from him.
"I don't blame yer," he gulped at last. "I wouldn't pass my own self on my answers, but I give yer my word that so far as I've had any religion, it's been all the religion I've had. For God's sake, let me sit in Lodge again, Brother!"
When the examinations were ended, a Lodge Officer came round with our aprons — no tinsel or silver-gilt confections, but heavily-corded silk with tassels and — where a man could prove he was entitled to them —

levels, of decent plate. Some one in front of me tightened a belt on a stiffly silent person in civil clothes with discharge-badge. " 'Strewth! This is comfort again," I heard him say. The companion nodded. The man went on suddenly: "Here! What're you doing? Leave off! You promised not to! Chuck it!" and dabbed at his companion's streaming eyes.

"Let him leak," said an Australian signaller. "Can't you see how happy the beggar is?"

He does not seem to have looked with any confidence to Christianity for the consolation and assurance that he needed. There are signs that he was attracted by another religion, one which had already disappeared from the earth when our civilisation was only just beginning to take shape. Valens, in *The Church that Was at Antioch* (has anyone ever noticed by the way that this story is virtually an austerer repetition of *Only a Subaltern?*) follows Mithras because he "wants more" than the official Roman religion. But Mithraism makes a much earlier appearance in Kipling's work than this. Parnesius, in *Puck of Pook's Hill,* first came to know his friend Pertinax "at a ceremony in our Temple — in the dark. It was the Bull Killing. . . . In the Cave we first met, and we were both raised to the Degree of Gryphons together." It was to this story that Kipling attached his *Song to Mithras:*

Sunset and After-Glow

Mithras, God of the Morning, our trumpets waken the Wall!
"Rome is above the Nations, but Thou art over all!"
Now as the names are answered, and the guards are marched away,
Mithras, also a soldier, give us strength for the day!

No doubt the fact that Mithraism was essentially a military religion and was widespread through the armies of the Empire goes some way to explain the attraction it held for Kipling. But there was another reason, which is betrayed in the words of Parnesius. It had also something of the character of a semi-secret society, with initiations, and degrees of advancement and ceremonies which were guarded from all but the initiates of the proper degree. This appealed to something very deep in Kipling's nature. It engendered, he felt, an intimacy of strength and co-operation which satisfied a craving in him. And it was in fact a mature version of the mysteries and catchwords by means of which Beetle, Stalky and Turkey distinguished themselves from the alien, uninitiated world outside Study Five.

IV

In spite of all this sometimes tortured searching and groping, Kipling's last book, which came somewhat unexpectedly after his death in the shape of some chapters of autobiography, has a peculiar serenity. "Looking back", it begins, "from this my seventieth year, it seems to me that every card in my working life has been dealt me in such a manner that I had but to play it as it came." And this may be regarded as the last word on a life which, for all its two poignant domestic sorrows (to neither of which does Kipling allude in this narrative), was as happy as it was well-filled.

Now that this life has been over for more than four years, we may ask ourselves what it has left behind it. As this essay was approaching its end I read a book by Mr. Malcolm Elwin called *Old Gods Falling*. It purports to be a study of the writers, principally writers of fiction, of the end of the last century and the beginning of this but it devotes little space either to Kipling's work or to his influence. What little it does devote contains that which, I confess, surprised me. Here is a specimen:

Both Haggard and Kipling wrote tales of adventure for boys, both lacked skill in drawing character, both wrote more rapidly than was good for them, both possessed in an extraordinary degree the gift of narrative, and both had vivid imaginations, though Haggard's exceeded Kipling's in the ingenuity, variety and daring of its range.

Sunset and After-Glow

Mr. Elwin further remarks that:

> Kipling was not original even in his glorification of "slicing and potting," for Rider Haggard was pre-eminently the novelist of "Blood," and *King Solomon's Mines* appeared a year before *Plain Tales from the Hills*.

He also describes Kipling's poetry as "jingling doggerel".

This is no doubt an extreme example of the treatment Kipling sometimes receives from the younger critics. It arises, I should imagine, from ignorance rather than from a perverted judgement. One may or may not give Kipling a high place in literature, but it would appear impossible for any critic who has read *The Man Who Would Be King* or *The Wish House* to dismiss him as merely a writer of "tales of adventure for boys". Similarly it is surely impossible for a critic who has read *Cities and Thrones and Powers* or *To Lalage* to consider his poetry no more than "jingling doggerel".

But the question remains whether an opinion resembling Mr. Elwin's is likely to prevail. Certainly the causes which raised political prejudice against Kipling have not been removed. If he did glorify war, there are more people than ever, in the English-speaking world, at any rate, who detest such a glorification. And the authoritarianism which he did undoubtedly preach, the ideal of the "strong man ruling alone", is looked at askance by most of us. When the "democratic countries" are rallying all their forces, both physical and moral, to meet the "dictator countries", there must be some prejudice against a writer who could never see a democratic institution without wanting to heave half a brick at it.

With the charge that Kipling glorified war for its own sake I have already dealt at some length. If he ever did, and I do not think that he did, save in a few moments of unguarded exuberance, assuredly he recanted before he was very old. (It is true of course that he did frequently extol the virtues, courage, fidelity, self-sacrifice, which flourish in war, but there is no evidence that he held war to be justified by its promotion of them.)

I have also endeavoured to elucidate the true nature of his authoritarianism. This did not extend to any fundamental sympathy with the totalitarian state as we now see it on the Continent. Of this there is one significant indication. For many years all his books bore the swastika as a sort of trade-mark. But when the Nazi Party came into power in Germany, and it became the symbol of the German nation as well as of

Sunset and After-Glow

the Nazi philosophy, he discontinued its use. This was not because of any patriotic jealousy of the revival of German power. It was because the Nazi philosophy was in its essence abhorrent to him. Above all things he believed in the reign of law, supreme over great and small alike, and to this the methods of Nazism seemed to him to offer an ultimate and evil challenge. When he saw them enthroned he experienced again the same sensations which he had expressed in 1914. Once more the Hun was at the gate, threatening "the ages' slow-bought gain", that civilisation of peace and order of which, throughout his life, Kipling was as much the devoted servant as either of his young men on the Wall.

The true basis of his authoritarianism lies in the principle: "Give the job to the man who can do it and let him do it without inexpert interference". In this way, he believed, and only in this way, could the "ages' slow-bought gain" be preserved and augmented. In a sense it may almost be said that his serious work consists of one exemplification after another of this master principle. We must admit that he never very clearly explained who was to choose the experts or, if it were that "strong man ruling alone", how he himself was to be chosen. Presumably in a world

Rudyard Kipling

in which Kipling's doctrine prevailed the right men would choose themselves for all positions by reason of their manifest fitness.

Ultimately his political ideal was anarchy, the Marxist withering away of the state. He wrote his Utopia and, if an author is not to be believed in his Utopia, then where is he to be believed? In his Utopia he shows us a way of life in which there is a minimum of governmental interference. In this way of life people do not scramble for positions of authority. They rather shirk them — and here, to be sure, is a sign of weakness in Kipling's scheme of things. The ideal state he envisages might well go to ruin because of the desire, and the admitted right, of every individual in it to attend to his own private affairs and let everything else go as it may. There must be many stages of development between Kipling's world and Kipling's Utopia.

And we must remember that he was a poet, who presented what he had to say in the form of images. He rarely spoke directly to any audience. His few public speeches, preserved in *A Book of Words*, show him, as always, anxious to present his argument, if not in the form of a story, at any rate in that of vivid images. But, in spite of that, he was quite capable of presenting his philosophy when he thought fit. This is an ex-

Sunset and After-Glow

tract from a speech he made to the students of Middlesex Hospital in 1907:

I do not think I need stretch your patience by talking to you about the high ideals and lofty ethics of a profession which exacts from its followers the largest responsibility and the highest death-rate — for its practitioners — of any profession in the world. If you will let me, I will wish you in your future what all men desire — enough work to do, and strength enough to do the work.

What all men desire! In that phrase and its explanation lies the heart of what Kipling had it in him to say. It is an inspiring doctrine, capable, as he showed, of rich and varied exemplification. For what doctrine has to do with it, we may safely prophesy that his work will not go stale.

When we consider him as an artist, it is again of his richness and his variety that we must first think. His stories hold a world. It may be objected that the creatures in this world are not the three-dimensional flesh-and-blood creatures whom we find in the great novelists. That is of course inevitable with the writer of short stories, though it may be added that it was probably his lack of the ability to develop a character patiently and in detail which turned him to the short story rather than to the novel. But it will

Rudyard Kipling

not be denied that, within the limits of the form, his power of depicting character is remarkable. He brings his characters at once to the eye in those few sentences which the form prescribes. Take as random examples the unhappy Miss Sichliffe in *The Dog Hervey,* choosing a puppy from the litter:

Attley turned to a dark, sallow-skinned, slack-mouthed girl, who had come over from tennis, and invited her to pick. She put on a pair of pince-nez that made her look like a camel, knelt clumsily, for she was long from the hip to the knee, breathed hard, and considered the last couple.

The District Nurse in *The Wish House,* interrupting the old village women who are discussing a tempestuous past:

The young lady entered briskly, all the bottles in her bag clicking. "Evenin', Mrs. Ashcroft," she began. "I've come raound a little earlier than usual because of the Institute dance to-na-ite. You won't ma-ind, will you?"

"Oh, no. Me dancin' days are over." Mrs. Ashcroft was the self-contained domestic at once. "My old friend, Mrs. Fettley 'ere, has been settin' talkin' with me a while."

"I hope she 'asn't been fatiguing you?" said the Nurse a little frostily.

"Quite the contrary. It 'as been a pleasure. Only

Sunset and After-Glow

— only — just at the end I felt a bit — a bit flogged out like."

"Yes, yes." The Nurse was on her knees already with the washes to hand. "When old ladies get together they talk a deal too much, I've noticed."

Then there is the odd little scene between Napoleon and Talleyrand in *A Priest in Spite of Himself:*

> He stamped about and swore at Talleyrand.
> "You forget yourself, Consul," says Talleyrand, "or rather you remember yourself — Corsican."
> "Pig!" says Boney, and worse.
> "Emperor!" says Talleyrand, but, the way he spoke, it sounded worst of all.
> . . . He [Napoleon] was a lanky-haired, yellow-skinned little man, as nervous as a cat — and as dangerous. I could feel that.

I have taken these examples, as I say, at random but with one reservation, that they are not among Kipling's famous characters. It is hardly necessary to say that he has impressed his three schoolboys, his three soldiers, Strickland, McPhee, and a score more on the memories of now nearly two generations of readers.

It has been a temptation to add something more, with illustrative quotations, which it would be a joy to transcribe, about the settings of his stories, his lovely landscapes. But instead I ask

Rudyard Kipling

the reader to turn back the pages for pictures I have already given. The same desire, to speak once more of Kipling's poetry, I equally suppress, for the same reason.

But let me consider again, before I leave the book on which I have spent more than three enjoyable years, the wide and various world which has been its subject. Wide and various indeed — soldiers and civilians in India. Lalun in *On the City Wall*, whose "very-great-grandmamma" was Lilith and who was married to a jujube-tree, the boys and masters of the United Services College, "Brugglesmith", wolves, bears and pythons in the jungle, seals in the southern oceans, horses in a New England pasture, the ghost-children of *They*, the young men who held the Wall against the barbarians, Hobden, who appears also as Hobdenius, and Mrs. Ashcroft, who said, through the letter-box to the Token in the Wish House, "Let me take everythin' bad that's in store for my man, 'Arry Mockler, for love's sake". And then there is Rahere, the jester of Henry I, who makes many appearances in prose and in verse. Rahere should be studied by those who wish to understand Kipling's method of writing, adopted in his middle years, so that the same piece could mean different things to different readers and different things to the same reader at different times. He should be

Sunset and After-Glow

studied also by those who wish to understand Kipling's inmost thoughts on the governance of mankind.

This perfunctory catalogue may give some idea of the world which I have been attempting to describe. I hope that it will also suggest the extensions of that world in other dimensions. Kipling's life provides a remarkable example of the artist who is not content to go on doing what he has already done well, of the artist whose style changes with that changing view of the world which it exists to express.

PR
4856   Shanks
.S5   Rudyard Kipling
1970

Date Due

JAN 1 0 1978			
MAY 2 2 1979			
MAR 1 5 1983			

Concordia College Library
Bronxville, New York 10708